50 Great Irish Drinking Songs

ROBERT GOGAN

Music Ireland

Published by Music Ireland, Ballymacmorris, Kilbeggan, County Westmeath, Ireland

"Fiddlers Green": © Hedley Music Group, PO Box 150, Chesterfield, Derbyshire S40 OYT, England

Designed and compiled by Robert Gogan
Cover/CD design by Ed McGinley, Dublin

Photographs
Front cover photograph - "Ballad singer" by Kate Horgan, Dublin
Back cover photograph by Robert Gogan
Internal photographs - Robert Gogan and Anne Tyrrell

CD
Recorded at Sonic Studios, Dublin
Engineer: Al Cowan
Produced by Robert Gogan

Musicians
John Doyle (Vocals)
Roddy Gallagher (Guitar)
Robert Gogan (Vocals/guitar)

www.goganbooks.com

ISBN   978 0 9532068 4 1

Mac's Bar, Bunratty Folk Park, Clare

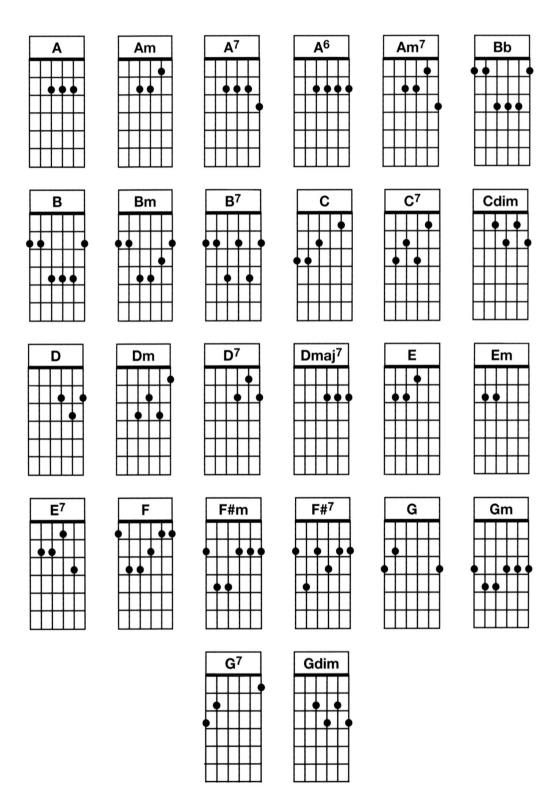

Introduction

The Irish, they say, will break into song at the drop of a hat.
And indeed many of them, they also say, will take a jar at the drop of a hat!
These two observations are very often intertwined.
In this selection of Drinking Songs I have collected together an assortment of well known ballads, mainly on the subject of 'the drink'. I have also included a number of my favourite Irish ballads - the ones that are most often 'broken into' when there might be a jar on board!
So enjoy these ballads - they are crying out to be sung. Drink or no drink!

A Big Thank You

There are many people who encouraged and helped me with this book.
I would like to thank Trish Ryan, Sharon Murphy, Dec "I'll get this C diminished to work if it kills me" O'Brien and Karen O'Mahony formerly of the Mechanical Copyright Protection Society.
I also wish to thank my partner Anne Tyrrell for putting up with me as I compiled this book, making some very useful suggestions and taking some of the photographs included in this book. Her patience and enthusiasm were an inspiration to me!
I am also most grateful to my good friend, historian and author Éamonn MacThomáis, now sadly no longer with us. Over long conversations as we drove and strolled around Dublin Éamonn would explain to me in great detail the local backgrounds to some of the great Irish ballads and I am delighted to be able to pass on his knowledge and wisdom in this book.
The following books and websites were also of great assistance:-
"The Petrie Collection of Ancient Music of Ireland" edited by David Cooper. Cork University Press
"The Irish Music Manuscripts of Edward Bunting (1773 - 1843). An Introduction and Catalogue" edited by Colette Moloney. Irish Traditional Music Archive.
"Folksongs of Britain and Ireland" edited by Peter Kennedy. Cassell
"The Complete Guide to Celtic Music" by June Skinner Sawyers. Aurum Press
"The Age of Revolution in the Irish Song Tradition 1776 - 1815" edited by Terry Moylan. Lilliput Press
"Irish Ballads" edited by Fleur Robertson. Gill & MacMillan
"The Poolbeg Book of Irish Ballads" by Sean McMahon. Poolbeg Press
"The Oxford Companion to Irish History" edited by S.J. Connolly. Oxford University Press
"AA Illustrated Road Book of Ireland" Automobile Association
"The Encyclopaedia of Ireland" edited by Brian Lalor. Gill & McMillan
"The World of Percy French" by Brendan O'Dowda. Blackstaff Press
"In Praise of Poteen" by John McGuffin. Appletree Press
"From Bawnboy and Templeport: History Heritage and Folklore" by Chris Maguire
www.contemplator.com/folk
www.mudcat.org
www.standingstones.com
www.geocities.com/shantysong
www.mysongbook.de
And also "The John Creedon Show" RTE Radio 1

The Chorus

If a song has a chorus it is printed in bold italics *like this*. Some songs start with a chorus and therefore it will be in the main body of the score. Others have the chorus after the first verse.
Choruses are great things - they are a law unto themselves. You can add more in (and this normally depends on the number of verses of the ballad you know!) or take them out if you want to shorten the song.

So do your own thing! Sing them *your* way - that's what ballads are all about!

Robert Gogan

The Hallowed Ground! Main entrance to the Guinness Brewery, James's Street, Dublin

Guinness Stout

The name of Guinness and the familiar Irish harp trade mark are without doubt international emblems of Ireland. Whenever I travel abroad and mention that I'm from Ireland the typical instant reaction is "ah yes, Guinness!"

And then I get homesick and have to come home!

Arthur Guinness (1725 - 1803) was the son of a land agent. He established a brewing business at Leixlip in County Kildare in 1756.

On December 31st 1759 he took over Mark Rainsford's Ale Brewery, a rundown ill-equipped brewery on Dublin's James's Street. He signed a lease for the property for 9,000 years at £45 per annum.

The brewing industry was a difficult one in those days. There were about 70 small breweries located in Dublin, and beer was virtually unknown in rural Ireland where the staple tipple was whiskey, gin or poteen.

Arthur Guinness (or Uncle Arthur as he is affectionately known) was well aware of the difficulties facing him. He was aware that his products were pretty mediocre and that the prevailing trade regulations favoured the London Porter breweries.

Nevertheless brewing could be a highly profitable business and the 34 year old Arthur was determined to have his slice of the cake.

However the Dublin breweries were under threat from a new beer brewed in London and recently introduced to the Dublin market. This unusual beer contained roasted barley which gave it a naturally dark colour and unique flavour. It was known as 'porter' because it was very popular among the porters and stevedores of London's Covent Garden and Billingsgate.

So Uncle Arthur had to make an important decision: should he stick with the traditional Dublin ales, or challenge the London breweries by brewing porter himself.

Thank God he made the right decision! He was so successful at brewing the dark rich beer that he ousted all porter imports from the Irish market and actually exported his beer into England.

In the early 1820's the beer became known as "stout porter". An "extra stout porter" was also produced - this was stronger and more robust than the original.

The word "stout" quickly became a name in its own right, as did the name "Guinness".

By 1838 the Guinness St. James's Street Brewery was the largest in Ireland.

In 1881 the annual production of Guinness exceeded one million barrels and in 1914 St. James's Gate became the world's largest brewery.

St. James's Gate is no longer the largest brewery in the world, but it is still the largest stout brewery.

Guinness is now brewed in 35 countries worldwide. However the flavoured extract is still exported from St. James's Gate to each of these breweries.

Guinness is so popular in Ireland that if you call for 'a pint' in your local pub without specifying the beer you want, you will automatically be provided with a pint of Guinness.

90,000 tonnes of Irish grown barley is used in the Guinness brewery each year - this represents 7% of the entire Irish crop. The vast bulk of this barley intake is germinated and dried to produce malt, which is the main ingredient of Guinness.

10,000 tonnes of barley is roasted each year to produce the unique colour and flavour of Guinness. A further 10,000 tonnes of barley each year is steamed and rolled (like porridge oats). This, together with the roasted barley and the malt, form the grist. Added to this is the hops, to give bitterness, aroma and preservative qualities. Over ten million glasses of Guinness are enjoyed each day throughout the world.

The daily production at the James's Gate Brewery is four million pints.

Now that's what I call a lot of stout!

My only big worry is: if the Guinness lease is only for 9,000 years from 1759, then what are we going to do when the lease runs out in 8,754 year's time??

It keeps me awake at night.

Percy French (1854 - 1920)

William Percy French was born in the quiet townland of Cloonyquin in County Roscommon. His family were prosperous landowners and Willie (as he was known in his early years) enjoyed a priviledged childhood.

He entered Trinity College Dublin in 1872 to study Civil Engineering and it took him so long to complete the course that he still retains the record for the student who took the longest time to obtain such a degree at that educational institution.

Instead of applying himself to his studies in Trinity College Willie French devoted his time to writing songs and poems, dramatics, watercolour painting and banjo playing.

In 1883 he obtained a post on a government drainage scheme in County Cavan and christened himself the 'Inspector of Drains'.

While serving in Cavan he bought himself a bicycle and lazily travelled far and wide, absorbing the characters he met and the conversations he overheard. During this time he wrote many pieces, including the well known "Phil the Fluther's Ball", and "Slathery's Mounted Fut".

When the Board of Works decided to reduce staff French was dismissed. He was seriously short of funds, as all the money which he had managed to save had been invested in a distillery which also failed around the same time.

In 1889 he was appointed editor of a new weekly comic paper "The Jarvey" which described itself as 'The Irish Punch'.

In 1890 he married Ethel (Ettie) Moore and in spite of both of their efforts "The Jarvey" ceased publication in 1891.

He was useless at financial planning and realised in early 1891 that his now pregnant wife and himself were in poor circumstances. On June 29th, the day following their first wedding anniversary, Ettie died in childbirth. The baby only survived a few weeks.

Some weeks prior to that French had collaborated with William Houston Collisson to write a musical entitled "The Knight of the Road" later renamed "The Irish Girl". It was very successful and things were looking up for French when poor Ettie died.

In 1894 French married his second wife, Helen (Lennie) Sheldon who bore him three daughters - Ettie, Mellie and Joan.

By this time French had turned to the stage for a full-time career and was winning widespread acclaim. He quickly became known by his stage name - Percy French. In 1900 he toured abroad with great success,

initially in Britain and later with his life-long colleague, Collisson, in Canada, USA and the West Indies.

The content of the shows was based around his own compositions, recitations, parodies and humorous sketches.

Although based in London from 1900 he returned each year to play the holiday resorts and towns of Ireland.

Many of French's best compositions were written with a view to inclusion in his own shows with scant consideration for future publication.

The touring revived his interest in watercolour painting which had lapsed for some time.

In spite of his many talents he always considered landscape painting to be his forte. When he would have a sufficient number of paintings completed he would arrange exhibitions in Dublin or London.

His painting expeditions into rural settings also provided material for his songs as he engaged with the local folk.

His reputation continued to grow and he performed for the Prince of Wales, later King Edward VII. He was very popular with the entire Royal Family and was commissioned to paint several pictures for them.

He continued to pursue his arduous itineraries into his sixties, and the tough life (though he never saw it as such) began to take its toll. He became ill in Formby, England and pneumonia was diagnosed. Just as he seemed to be recovering from this he died of heart failure on January 24th, 1920. He was buried in the peaceful St. Luke's graveyard in Formby.

Versatile, humble, quick-witted and much loved by everybody who knew him, the memory of Percy French lives on, particularly through his songs.

He managed to express the funny and quirky sides of rural Ireland without offending anybody. The characters in his songs are charming and funny and it is clear that French is not laughing *at* them - he is laughing *with* them. And the popularity of his shows throughout Ireland demonstrate that they fully understood that.

He had too much affection for them and this affection radiates throughout his songs, such as "Are You Right, There, Michael, Are You Right?", "The Darling Girl from Clare", "The Mountains of Mourne" and many more.

There are three Percy French songs in this book:-

"Come Back Paddy Reilly" (page 4)

"Eileen Óg" (page 28)

"Phil the Fluther's Ball" (page 64)

Site of Cloonyquin House, birthplace of Percy French, Roscommon

The Valley House, Achill Island, Mayo

This ballad is also known as "Molly Malone" and is without doubt the Dublin Anthem at all sporting events, and the unofficial National Anthem among all Irish people abroad.

I believe that the earliest known version of this ballad was published in London in 1884. It was described as a comic song (!) and was attributed to James Yorkston of Scotland. It was noted as "printed with permission" of an Edinburgh firm so there must have been an earlier version.

A Molly Malone was listed in the St Werburgh parish records as having died in 1734. She was buried in St John's churchyard at the top of Fishamble Street beside Christchurch Cathedral. As a fishmonger she probably lived around this area, Fishamble Street owing its name to a medieval fish market which was held there many years ago. In those days fish was sold in markets and also by street traders who pushed their goods through the streets of Dublin on two-wheeled carts.

The word 'shamble' is an old English word for a market-place or market stall (hence, 'Fishamble' Street). These market-places are usually quite messy or cluttered. This word has filtered down through the ages and the word 'shambles' now indicates a general mess. So the next time you're told that your car, or office or hair (or life!) is 'in a complete shambles', at least you'll know where the word came from!

There is a wonderful bronze statue of the mythical Molly Malone at the junction of Grafton, Nassau and Suffolk Streets, beside Trinity College in Dublin. It is not unknown for visitors to Dublin to toss coins into the cleft of her ample bosom and make a wish!

This is a 'must learn' ballad if you wish to take part in any Irish ballad sessions anywhere in the world.

She was a fishmonger and sure 'twas no wonder
For so was her father and mother before
And they both wheeled their barrows through streets broad and narrow
Crying "Cockles and mussels, alive, alive-oh!" *Chorus*

She died of a fever and no one could save her
And that was the end of sweet Molly Malone
Now her ghost wheels her barrow through streets broad and narrow
Crying "Cockles and mussels, alive, alive-oh!" *Chorus*

Johnnie Fox's, Glencullen, Dublin mountains

This ballad is an excerpt from an old capstan sea shanty which contained up to nineteen verses in some versions. The reference to 'Valiporazor' (Valiparaiso) in Chile suggests that it probably originated in Liverpool as there was much trade between the two ports.

The capstan (or windlass) shanties were used for long and repetitive tasks, one of the main ones being the raising and lowering of the anchor, when the winding and unwinding was carried out by sailors walking round and round pushing at the capstan bars.

For more information on sea shanties. See "The Holy Ground" - page 80.

Now some of our fellows had been drinking; and me meself was heavy on the booze
So I sat upon me old sea chest a-thinking; I'll just turn in and have meself a snooze
Well I wished that I was in the Jolly Sailors; along with Irish Paddys drinking beer
Then I thought of what a jolly lot are sailors; and with me flipper I wiped away a tear. **Chorus**

Well when we gathered all the tugs alongside; they towed us from the wharf and out to sea
With half the crew a hanging o'er the ship's side; the bloody row that started sickened me
The bowsen he said that he couldn't savvy; the crew were speaking lingoes all galore
So the only thing the old man he could do was; just pay us sailors off and ship some more. **Chorus**

Come Back Paddy Reilly

This beautiful melodic song comes from the pen of Percy French.

While French was working as a Civil Engineer for the Board of Works in the 1880's he was appointed to work on a particular scheme in County Cavan, a border county between the Irish Republic and Northern Ireland.

He would frequently take the train up to the town of Ballyjamesduff and be collected at the station by his cabman, Paddy Reilly.

In or around 1913 Frency paid a return visit to Ballyjamesduff and was saddened to hear that Paddy Reilly had emigrated. He wrote this song to mark the occassion.

Ballyjamesduff is a village in County Cavan not far from Lough Sheelin. It was named after Sir James Duff, an English officer in the 1798 Insurrection.

In this song French mentions various towns and places located in Cavan.

Further information on Percy French is to be found at the front of this book.

My mother once told me that when I was born
The day that I first saw the light
I looked down the street on that very first morn
And gave a great crow of delight
Now most new-born babies appear in a huff
And start with a sorrowful squall
But I know I was born down in Ballyjamesduff
And that's why I smile on them all
The baby's a man now, he's toil-worn and tough
Still whispers from over the sea
"Come back Paddy Reilly to Ballyjamesduff
Come home Paddy Reilly to me".

The night that we danced by the light of the moon
With Phil to the fore with his flute
When Phil threw his lip over "Come again soon"
He'd dance the foot out of your boot
The day that I took Long Magee by the scruff
For slanderin Rosie Kilrain
Then marchin' him straight out of Ballyjamesduff
Assisted him into a drain
Oh sweet are me dreams as the dudeen I puff
Of whisperings over the sea
"Come back Paddy Reilly to Ballyjamesduff
Come home Paddy Reilly to me".

I've loved the young women of every land
That always came easy to me
Just barrin' the belles of the Blackamore brand
And chocolate shapes of Feegee
But that sort of stuff is a moon-shining stuff
And never will addle me brain
For bells will be ringin' in Ballyjamesduff
For me and me Rosie Kilrain
And all through their glamour, their gass and their guff
A whisper comes over the sea
"Come back Paddy Reilly to Ballyjamesduff
Come home Paddy Reilly to me".

Aughrim, Galway

Courtin' In The Kitchen

This Dublin ballad probably dates from the early 19th century.

"Courting" is a quaint Irish verb which means, in its broadest sense, to "get romantically involved with". It would cover every activity from holding hands, to gentle kissing, to a whole lot of other things!

There is a reference in this ballad to "Stephen's Green" which is situated in the heart of Dublin. St. Stephen's Green was originally a common in the 17th century and became a Square for the exclusive use of surrounding residents in the 18th century. It is now a beautiful 22 acre park, open to the public.

A "Repealer's Coat" was a greatcoat which sported a badge showing that the wearer was a supporter of Daniel O'Connell and his movement for the repeal of the Act of Union and the restoration of a separate Irish Parliament.

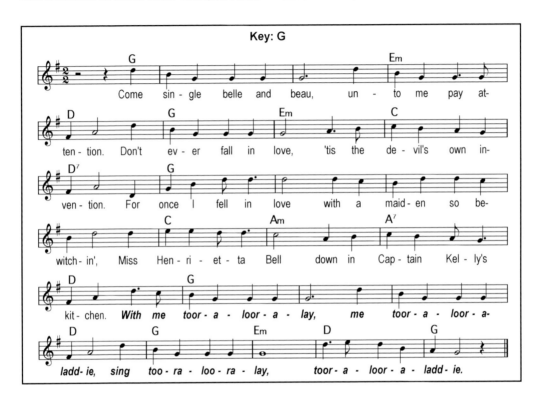

At the age of seventeen I was 'prenticed to a grocer
Not far from Stephen's Green where Miss Henri' used to go sir
Her manners were so fine; she set me heart a-twitchin'
When she asked meself to tea down in Captain Kelly's kitchen.
Chorus

Now Sunday being the day when we were to have the flare-up
I dressed meself quite gay and I frizzed and oiled me hair up
The Captain had no wife and he'd gone off a-fishin'
So we kicked up the high life out of sight down in the kitchen.
Chorus

Just as the clock struck six we sat down at the table
She handed tea and cakes and I ate what I was able
I had cakes with punch and tay till me side it got a stitch in
And the time it passed away with the courtin' in the kitchen.
Chorus

With me arms around her waist she slyly hinted marriage
When through the door in haste we heard Captain Kelly's carriage
Her eyes told me full well, and they were not bewitchin'
That she wished I'd get to hell, or be somewhere from that kitchen.
Chorus

She flew up off her knees, some five feet up or higher
And over head and heels threw me slap into the fire
My new Repealer's coat that I got from Mr. Mitchel
With a twenty shilling note went to blazes in the kitchen.
Chorus

I grieved to see me duds all smeared with smoke and ashes
When a tub of dirty suds right into me face she dashes
As I lay on the floor and the water she kept pitchin'
Till a footman broke the door and came chargin' to the kitchen.
Chorus

When the Captain came downstairs, though he seen me situation
Despite of all my prayers I was marched off to the station
For me they'd take no bail, though to get home I was itchin'
And I had to tell the tale of how I came into the kitchen.
Chorus

I said she did invite me but she gave a flat denial
For assault she did indict me and meself was sent for trial
She swore I robbed the house in spite of all her screechin'
And I got six months hard for me courtin' in the kitchen.
Chorus

Lynott's Pub, Achill Island, Mayo

Crinkle, Offaly

This ballad is also known as 'The Rare Old Mountain Dew' and is attributed to Samuel Lover (1797 - 1869). It's about that much-loved of Irish beverages - 'poitín', or poteen, also known as moonshine, or mountain dew.

For more information about poitín and illicit distilleries see page 34
For other ballads about poitín, see "The Moonshiner" - page 66, and "Hills of Connemara" - page 35.

Key: G

Let the grass-es grow and the wat-ers flow in a free and eas-y way, but give me en-ough of the rare old stuff that's made near Gal-way Bay. And po-lice-men all from Do-ne-gal, Sli-go and Leit-rim too. We'll give them the slip and we'll take a sip of the rare old moun-tain dew.

At the foot of the hill there's a neat little still where the smoke curls up to the sky
By a whiff of a smell you can plainly tell there's a poitín still nearby
Oh it fills the air with a perfume rare and betwixt both me and you
As home we roll we can drink a bowl or a bucket of mountain dew. *Chorus*

Now learned men who use the pen have wrote the praises high
Of the sweet poitín from Ireland green distilled from wheat and rye
Away with pills, it'll cure all ills of Pagan, Christian or Jew
So take off your coat and grease your throat with the real old mountain dew. *Chorus*

Rathdrum, Wicklow

Preab San Ól (Another Round)

This is a wonderful lilting song about life in general in which the singer urges his listeners to forget about amassing wealth and to enjoy a few jars instead. A man after me own heart!

The late Luke Kelly of The Dubliners sang a superb version of this ballad. A 'florin' is the old Irish name for a two shilling coin.

King Solomon's glory, so famed in story, was far outshone by the lily's guise
But hard winds harden both field and garden, pleading for pardon, the lily dies
Life's but a bauble of toil and trouble, the feathered arrow, once shot ne'er found
So, lads and lasses, because life passes, come fill your glasses for another round.

The huckster greedy, he blinds the needy, their strife's unheeding, shouts "money down!"
These special vices, his fancy prices, for a florin value he'll charge a crown.
With hump for trammel, the scripture's camel missed needle's eye and so came to ground.
Why pine for riches, while still you've stitches to hold your britches up? Another round!

Thomas O'Connor, well-known Irish ballad singer, in full flight.
Yes, you're right, that is a black ladies bra on his head - the
result of a competition which he ran among the audience.
And I'm not saying any more!!

Seven Drunken Nights

This bawdy but very clever ballad became an international hit for the ballad group The Dubliners in 1967 and it is still extremely popular at ballad sessions to the present day.

It certainly encourages the theory that many's an Irishman has more of an interest in drink than he has in the fairer sex!

The ballad was collected by the collector Francis J. Child (1825 - 1896) under the title 'Our Goodman', where the drunken narrator only outlines five nights. It appears that the other two 'nights' were added much later!

In Ronnie Drew's introduction to the Dubliner's hit he says, "This song is called Seven Drunken Nights but we're only allowed sing five."

I too feel that I'm in the same boat.

You don't need to be a rocket scientist to work out where this song in going, and the last two verses are rather, eh, raunchy.

But fear not! You don't have to be denied the pleasure (!) of the final two verses.

They are available extensively on the internet

Key: C

As I came home on Mon-day night, as drunk as drunk can be, I saw a horse out-side the door where my old horse should be. Well I called my wife and I said to her would you kind-ly tell to me, who owns that horse out-side the door where my old horse should be. "Ah you're drunk, you're drunk, you sil-ly old fool, still you can-not see. That's a lov-e-ly sow that my moth-er sent to me". Well it's man-y's a day I've trav-elled, a hun-dred miles or more, but a sad-dle on_ a sow, sure I've nev-er seen be-fore

And as I came home on Tuesday night as drunk as drunk could be
I saw a coat behind the door where my old coat should be
Well I called me wife and I said to her, "Would you kindly tell to me
Who owns that coat behind the door where my old coat should be"
"Ah, you're drunk, you're drunk you silly old fool, still you cannot see
That's a woollen blanket that me mother sent to me"
Well, it's many's a day I've travelled a hundred miles or more
But buttons in a blanket sure I never saw before.

And as I came home on Wednesday night as drunk as drunk could be
I saw a pipe upon the chair where my old pipe should be
Well I called me wife and I said to her, "Would you kindly tell to me
Who owns that pipe upon the chair where my old pipe should be"
"Ah, you're drunk, you're drunk you silly old fool, still you cannot see
That's a lovely tin whistle that me mother sent to me"
Well, it's many's a day I've travelled a hundred miles or more
But tobacco in a tin whistle sure I never saw before.

And as I came home on Thursday night as drunk as drunk could be
I saw two boots beneath the bed where my old boots should be
Well I called me wife and I said to her, "Would you kindly tell to me
Who owns them boots beneath the bed where my old boots should be"
"Ah, you're drunk, you're drunk you silly old fool, still you cannot see
They're two lovely Geranium pots me mother sent to me"
Well, it's many's a day I've travelled a hundred miles or more
But laces in Geranium pots I never saw before.

And as I came home on Friday night as drunk as drunk could be
I saw a head upon the bed where my old head should be
Well I called me wife and I said to her, "Would you kindly tell to me
Who owns that head upon the bed where my old head should be"
"Ah, you're drunk, you're drunk you silly old fool, still you cannot see
That's a baby boy that me mother sent to me"
Well, it's many's a day I've travelled a hundred miles or more
But a baby boy with his whiskers on sure I never saw before.

Ardrahan, Galway

This great Dublin ballad was written by George Hodnett and is quite bawdy, using Dublin slang words and 'double meaning' to paint a colourful picture.

"Monto" is a colloquial abbreviation for Montgomery Street which, along with Corporation Street, Railway Street and Foley Street (all located between the Custom House and O'Connell Bridge) formed one of the best known and largest red-light districts in Europe. At the beginning of the 20th century it is estimated that around 1800 prostitutes were operating in these streets. Montgomery Street was also considered at the time to be one of the worst slums in Western Europe.

The heyday of the area began in the middle of the 19th century when the district, then a fashionable group of streets, became home to two regiments of British soldiers. The women flocked to do 'business' there! This was the red-light district of gaslit, foggy and thronging streets.

The area was closed down and cleared of its night-time activities in 1925, following pressure from the citizens of Dublin.

Here are some interpretations for your better understanding of the ballad:-

"waxies" - either candle makers or those who waxed bootlaces. See "The Waxies' Dargle" - page 58; "mot"

- girlfriend; "Furry Glen" - this is a small glen in the Phoenix Park; "childer" - children; "Vicky" - Queen Victoria.

"Butcher Foster" refers to Chief Secretary Forster who introduced Coercion Acts in Ireland in the late 19th century which permitted the imprisonment of any person on the mere suspicion of being involved in criminal activity. He was very unpopular and was nicknamed 'Buckshot'.

"Invincibles" - Extremist Nationalist society with Fenian backgrounds devoted to political assassination. On May 6th 1882 The Dublin section carried out the assassination with surgical knives of the newly appointed Irish Chief Secretary Lord Frederick Cavendish and the Under-Secretary, T.H. Burke. The assassinations took place in Phoenix Park and the incident became known as 'The Phoenix Park murders'. 'Skin-the-Goat' was the nickname of James Fitzharris, the cabman who drove the Invincibles to the Park. One of the Invincibles, James Carey, was arrested and turned State's Evidence which led to the hanging of five of his comrades. Freed for his co-operation, Carey was later shot dead by an Invincible, Patrick O'Donnell, on board the ship 'The Melrose' travelling between Durban and Cape Town.

"Phoenix" - Phoenix Park; "Garda" - Irish police force; "Wearing of the Green" - well known Irish patriotic ballad.

You've heard of Butcher Foster the dirty old impostor
He took his mot and lost her up the Furry Glen
He first put on his bowler and he buttoned up his trousers
And he whistled for a growler and he said "My man.
*Chorus change: **Take me up to Monto, etc.***

You've heard the Dublin Fusiliers, the dirty old bamboozileers
They went and got their childer, one, two, three
They march them from the Linen Hall; there's one for every cannon ball
And Vicky's going to send them all o'er the sea.
*Chorus change: **But they'll first go up to Monto, etc.***

When Carey told on Skin-the-Goat, O'Donnell caught him on the boat
He wished he'd never been afloat, the dirty skite
It wasn't very sensible to tell on the Invincibles
They stuck up for the principles, day and night.
*Chorus change: **By going up to Monto, etc.***

When the Czar o' Roosha and the King o' Proosha
Landed in the Phoenix in a big balloon
They asked the Garda Band to play 'The Wearing of the Green'
But the buggers in the depot didn't know the tune.
*Chorus change: **So they took them up to Monto, etc.***

The Queen she came to call on us; she wanted to see all of us
I'm glad she didn't fall on us; she's eighteen stone
"Mister Mayor, melord", says she, "is that all you've got to show to me"
"Why no ma'am there's some more to see - póg mo thóin!"*
*Chorus change: **And he took her up to Monto, etc.***

Pronounced "Poag mo hoan". (Kiss my a - - e!)

**Having a pint and a chat
in Doheny & Nesbitt's,
Dublin**

The Galway Races

The main Galway Racing Festival, held on the Ballybrit Racecourse just outside Galway City on the west coast of Ireland takes place towards the end of July each year. The reference to "the seventeenth of August" in the ballad is a significant one because it was on August 17th, 1869 that the Ballybrit Racecourse was opened.

The Galway Racing Festival is one of the busiest and most popular festivals in the Irish festival calendar. The ballad gives the suggestion that the festival consisted of a lot more than just the racing and this is entirely true to this day. You will notice that the sixth verse is the only one which mentions anything about the actual races themselves!

I know several people who travel to the Galway Racing Festival every year and freely admit that they wouldn't see a horse from one end of the week to the other!

A "crubeen" is a boiled pig's foot. "Wattles" are small sticks and this is a reference to a Fair Attraction whereby participants would throw sticks at a moving target (in this case the hapless Maggie) and would I presume win a prize if they hit the target. "Fenian prisoners" refers to the daring rescue of six Fenian prisoners from the penal colonies in Australia on April 17th, 1876. The prisoners were successfully brought to the USA on board the whaler 'Catalpa', much to the embarrassment of the British authorities.

"Aran" refers to the Aran Islands off the west coast of Ireland which were much more heavily populated in the 19th century than they are today. "Connemara", "New Quay" and "Clare" are all located in the west of Ireland.

There were passengers from Limerick town and more from Tipperary
Boys from Connemara and the Clare unmarried maidens.
People from Cork City who were loyal, true and faithful
Who brought home the Fenian prisoners from dying in foreign nations. *Chorus*

It's there you'll see the gamblers, the thimbles and the garters
The sporting Wheel-of-Fortune with the four and twenty quarters
There were others without scruple pelting wattles at poor Maggie
And her daddy well contented to be gawking at his daughter. *Chorus*

It's there you'll see the pipers and the fiddlers competing
The nimble-footed dancers a-trippin' o'er the daisies
There were others crying "Cigars and lights" and "Bills for all the races"
With the colours of the jockeys and the price and horses' ages. *Chorus*

It's there you'll see confectioners with sugar sticks and dainties
The lozenges and oranges, the lemonade and raisins
The gingerbread and spices to accommodate the ladies
And a big crubeen for threepence to be sucking while you're able. *Chorus*

It's there you'll see the jockeys and they're mounted up so stately
The pink, the blue, the orange and green, the emblems of our nation
When the bell was rung for starting all the horses seemed impatient
I thought they never stood on ground their speed was so amazing. *Chorus*

There were half a million people there from all denominations
The Catholic, the Protestant, the Jew and Presbyterian
There was yet no animosity no matter what persuasion
But sportsmen's hospitality to induce fresh acquaintance. *(Repeat chorus twice)*

Galway City

Finnegan's Wake

This is a very popular Dublin ballad. Tim Finnegan lived in "Watling Street" which is situated in the heart of Dublin city not far from the famous Guinness brewery at James Gate. In the ballad Tim is a builder's labourer who is rather fond of booze.

Some versions of this ballad have Tim Finnegan living in "Walkin Street" but I can't find a Walkin Street in Dublin anywhere!

James Joyce took the title of this ballad for his final book "Finnegans Wake".

One morning Tim was rather full; his head felt heavy which made him shake
He fell off the ladder and he broke his skull and they carried him home his corpse to wake
They wrapped him up in a nice clean sheet and they laid him out upon the bed
With a bottle of whiskey at his feet and a barrel of porter at his head.
Chorus

His friends assembled at the wake and Mrs. Finnegan called for lunch
First she gave them tay and cake, then piped tobacco and brandy punch
Then the Widow Malone began to cry; such a lovely corpse she did ever see
"Yerra Tim mo bhourneen** why did you die"; "Will you hold your hour" said Molly Magee.
Chorus

Then Mary Murphy took up the job; "Yerra Biddy" says she "You're wrong, I'm sure"
Then Biddy fetched her a belt in the gob and left her sprawling on the floor
Civil war did then engage; woman to woman and man to man
Shillelagh law was all the rage and a row and a ruction soon began.
Chorus

Tim Moloney ducked his head when a bottle of whiskey flew at him
He ducked and, landing on the bed, the whiskey scattered over Tim
Well begob he revives and see how he's rising; Tim Finnegan rising in the bed
Saying "Fling your whiskey 'round like blazes! Be the thundering Jayses d'ye think I'm dead!"
Chorus

*Booze - usually whiskey
** Pronounced 'mo vourneen' (my loved one)

Killybegs, Donegal

(Verses and chorus have the same melody)

Botany Bay in Australia was originally known as Stingray Harbour. Located south of Sydney and its suburbs, a convict colony was established there by the English authorities in 1788. Therefore the name of Botany Bay became synonymous with penal colonies and punishment.

This ballad, however, is not the usual type of lament associated with Botany Bay and deportation. In this case the singer intends to travel to Botany Bay and make his fortune in Australia.

A 'navvy' was the term used for all labourers employed in the construction industry. The name originated at the time of the construction of artificial waterways and canals in England between the 17th and 19th centuries. These waterways were known as 'navigations'. The labourers who built these navigations were known as 'navigators', later abbreviated to 'navvy'. The name was soon applied to all construction workers.

The boss came up this morning, he says "Well Pat you know
If you don't get your navvies out I'm afraid you'll have to go"
So I asked him for my wages and demanded all my pay
For I told him straight I would emigrate to the shores of Botany Bay. ***Chorus***

And when I reach Australia I'll go and search for gold
There's plenty there for digging or so I have been told
Or else I'll go back to my trade and a hundred bricks I'll lay
Because I live for an eight hour shift on the shores of Botany Bay. ***Chorus***

A Flock of Pints? A Herd of Pints? No, it's a Pride of Pints!

(Verses and chorus have the same melody)

Keady is a small town in County Armagh (Northern Ireland) situated on high ground near the border with County Monaghan (Republic of Ireland).

This O'Donoghue fella seemed to fancy himself as a great catch for the ladies.

Please note that all Irishmen are not like that - most of us are bashful, polite, reserved, timid and humble - even if the women do chase us around all the time!

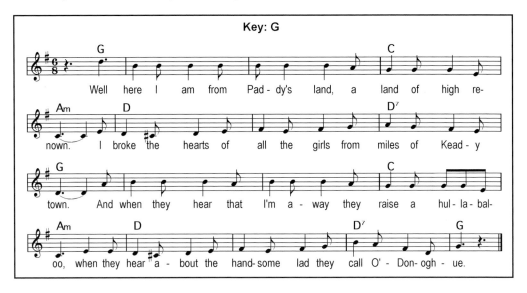

Key: G

Well here I am from Pad - dy's land, a land of high re-
nown. I broke the hearts of all the girls from miles of Kead - y
town. And when they hear that I'm a - way they raise a hul - la - bal-
oo, when they hear a - bout the hand-some lad they call O' - Don - ogh - ue.

For I'm the boy to please her and I'm the boy to tease her
I'm the boy to squeeze her and I'll tell you what I'll do
I'll court her like an Irishman with me brogue and blarney too
With me rollikin, swollikin, dollikin, wollikin bold O'Donoghue.

I wish me love was a red red rose growing on yonder wall
And me to be a dewdrop and upon her brow I'd fall
Perhaps now she might think of me as a rather heavy dew
No more she'd love the handsome lad they call O'Donoghue. ***Chorus***

They say that Queen Victoria has a daughter fine and grand
Perhaps she'd take it into her head for to marry an Irishman
And if I could only get a chance to have a word or two
Perhaps she'd take a notion in the Bold O'Donoghue! ***Chorus***

Lahinch, Clare

This modern song has assumed the mantle of a 'traditional ballad' due to its style and widespread popularity. It was written by John Conolly, a ballad singer who hails from Grimsby Town.

Now Fiddlers Green is a place I hear tell
Where fishermen go if they don't go to hell
Where the skies are all clear and the dolphins do play
And the cold coast of Greenland is far far away. *Chorus*

When you get to the docks and the long trip is through
And there's pubs and there's clubs and there's lassies there too
Where the girls are all pretty and the beer it is free
And there's bottles of rum hanging from every tree. *Chorus*

Now I don't want a harp nor a halo, not me
Just give me a breeze and a good rolling sea
I'll play me old squeezebox as we sail along
With the wind in the rigging to sing me a song. *Chorus*

This well-known ballad first appeared in print in 1904 and versions of it are to be found in Britain, Australia, Canada and the U.S.A.

In 1988 I won first prize in a talent competition on the "M.V. Orient Express" cruiser while on a cruising holiday in the Mediterranean - singing this ballad. The prize? A tee-shirt! I think I still have it somewhere.

It should have been the start of a brilliant career but, somehow, the recording contracts just didn't come in!

Key: G

I've been a wild rov-er for man-y's a year, and I've spent all my mon-ey on whis-key and beer. But now I'm ret-ur-ning with gold in great store, and I nev-er will play the wild rov-er no more. *And it's no nay nev-er, no nay nev-er no more, will I play the wild rov-er, no nev-er no more.*

I went into an alehouse I used to frequent
I told the landlady my money was spent
I asked her for credit, she answered me "Nay
Such custom as yours I can have any day". *Chorus*

I took out from my pocket ten sovereigns bright
And the landlady's eyes opened wide with delight
She said "I've got whiskeys and wines of the best
And the words that I spoke they were only in jest". *Chorus*

I'll go home to my parents, confess what I've done
And I'll ask them to pardon their prodigal son
And if they caress me as oft times before
Sure I never will play the wild rover no more. *Chorus*

Kenmare, Kerry

The Limerick Rake

This ballad is about a chap who certainly knows how to live life!

Limerick is a county located in the West of Ireland and there are references throughout the ballad to towns and places in Limerick and surrounding counties.

'John Damer' refers to a wealthy landlord who lived in the town of Shronel in County Tipperary in the mid 18th century and was very unpopular among the locals.

My parents had reared me to shake and to mow, to plough and to harrow, to reap and to sow
But my heart being airy to drop it so low, I set out on a high speculation
On paper and parchment they taught me to write; in Euclid and grammar they opened my eyes
And in multiplication in truth I was bright; yerra fágaimíd siúd mar atá sé.

If I chance for to go to the town of Rathkeale, the girls all round me do flock on the square
Some give me a bottle and others sweet cakes, and treat me unknown to their parents
There is one from Askeaton and one from the Pike, another from Arda, my heart was beguiled
Tho' being from the mountains her stockings are white, yerra fágaimíd siúd mar atá sé.

To quarrel for riches I ne'er was inclined, for the greatest of misers must leave them behind
I'll purchase a cow that will never run dry, and I'll milk her by twisting her horns
John Damer of Shronel had plenty of gold, and Devonshire's treasure is twenty times more
But he's laid on his back among nettles and stones, yerra fágaimíd siúd mar atá sé.

This cow can be milked without clover or grass, for she's pampered with corn, good barley and hops
She's warm and stout, and she's free in her paps, and she'll milk without spancil or halter
The man that will drink it will cock his caubeen, and if anyone coughs there'll be wigs on the green
And the feeble old hag will get supple and free, yerra fágaimíd siúd mar atá sé.

If I chance for to go to the market at Croom, with a cock in my hand and my pipes in full tune
I am welcome at once and brought up to a room, where Bacchus is sporting with Venus
There's Peggy and Jane from the town of Bruree, and Biddy from Bruff and we all on the spree
Such a combing of locks as there was about me, yerra fágaimíd siúd mar atá sé.

There's some say I'm foolish and more say I'm wise; to be fond of the women I think is no crime
The son of King David had ten thousand wives, and his wisdom was highly regarded
I'll take a good garden and live at my ease, and each woman and child can partake of the same
If there's war in the cabin, themselves they may blame, yerra fágaimíd siúd mar atá sé.

And now for the future I mean to be wise, and I'll send for the women that acted so kind
And I'll marry them all in the morn by and by, if the clergy'll agree to the bargain
And when I'm on my back and my soul is at peace, these women will crowd for to cry at my wake
And their sons and their dauhgters will offer their prayer, to the Lord for the soul of their father.

*Pronounced: "Fogameed shooed mar ataw shay". Difficult to translate literally, but the general gist is "Ah sure there y'are now!", or "that's the way things are!" or "Ah sure now ye have it!" And many more!

John Doyle, Irish ballad singer, and myself (the best banjo player in the world!) in The Temple Bar, Dublin

Spancil Hill

This ballad of emigration and homesickness is a favourite of all folk from County Clare and, indeed, throughout Ireland. Apparently there were eleven verses in the original song, but I only know seven of them. The ballad was written by Michael Considine, a native of Spancilhill Cross who emigrated to America in 1870 at the age of twenty. Considine was an articulate and intelligent young man who suffered from ill-health. He worked first in Boston but later moved to California - probably to avail of the better climate. He eventually qualified as an accountant and worked all his life in America. Towards the end of his life he wrote Spancilhill and sent it back to his nephew John Considine in Ireland. He died shortly afterwards.

The ballad was made famous by Robbie McMahon, a balladeer and native of Spancilhill.

Spancilhill Cross (to give it the correct name) is a crossroads situated to the east of the town of Ennis, the largest town in County Clare on the west coast of Ireland. Every year in June a week-long festival of horse, cattle and pony trading took place there. It is now held on just one day each June.

The last surviving daughter of "Tailor Quigley" died only a few years ago in Ennis.

Delighted by the novelty; enchanted with the scene
Where in my early boyhood where often I had been
I thought I heard a murmur and I think I hear it still
It's the little stream of water that flows down by Spancil Hill.

To amuse a passing fancy I lay down on the ground
And all my school companions were shortly gathered around
When we were home returning we would dance with bright goodwill
To Martin Moynihan's music at the cross at Spancil Hill.

It was on the twenty-third of June; the day before the fair
When Ireland's sons and daughters and friends assembled there
The young, the old, the brave and the bold, their duty to fulfil
At the parish church at Clooney, just a mile from Spancil Hill.

I went to see my neighbours and to hear what they might say
The old ones were all dead and gone; the young ones gone away
I met the tailor Quigley; he's as bold as ever still
Sure he used to mend my britches when I lived at Spancil Hill.

I paid a flying visit to my first and only love
She's as fair as any lily and as gentle as a dove
She threw her arms around me sayin' "Johnny I love you still"
For she was a farmer's daughter and the pride of Spancil Hill.

Well I dreamt I hugged and kissed her, as in the days of yore
She said "Johnny, you're only joking!"; as many's the time before
The cock she crew in the morning; she crew both loud and shrill
And I awoke in California, many miles from Spancil Hill.

Spancilhill Crossroads, Clare

Eileen Óg

(Chorus has the same melody as the last four lines of the verse)

This well known song about a disappointed suitor was written by Percy French in or around 1908.

The song is based in French's beloved west of Ireland. Ballintubber is a small village situated seven miles south of Castlebar in County Mayo.

Petravore is a townland near Swanlinbar in County Cavan, an area well known to Percy French. The local and official name of the area is Pedara Vohers, a translation from the Irish

'Peadair a bhóthair' (Peter's Road).

Petravore also appears in another of French's songs in this book - Phil the Fluther's Ball (page 64).

Whether or not 'Eileen' was a real person, or merely a figment of French's fertile imagine, is not known.

Further information on Perch French can be found at the front of this book.

Key: Dm

Eil - een Og, now that's the dar-lin's name is. Through the Bar-on-y her feat-ures they were fam-ous. If we loved her who was there to blame us, for sure was-n't she the Pride of Pet-rav-ore. But her beau - ty made us all so shy. Not a sin-gle man could look her in the eye. Boys, oh, boys, sure that's the reas-on why we're in mour-ning for the Pride of Pet - rav - ore!

Eileen Óg, me heart is going grey
Ever since the day you wandered far away
Eileen Óg, there's good fish in the say*
But there's none of them like the Pride of Petravore

Anybody thirsty?

Friday at the fair of Ballintubber
Eileen met McGrath the cattle jobber
I'd like to set me mark upon the robber
For he stole away the Pride of Petravore
He never seemed to see the girl at all
Even when she ogled him from underneath her shawl
Lookin' big and masterful when she was lookin' small
Most provokin' for the Pride of Petravore.
Chorus

So it went as 'twas in the beginning
Eileen Óg was bent upon the winning
Big McGrath contentedly was grinning
Being courted by the Pride of Petravore
Sez he: "I know a girl that could knock you into fits"
At that poor Eileen nearly lost her wits
The upshot of the ruction was that now the robber sits
With his arm around the Pride of Petravore.
Chorus

Boys, oh boys, with fate 'tis hard to grapple
Of my eye 'tis Eileen was the apple
Now to see her walkin' to the chapel
With the hardest featured man in Petravore
Now, boys, this is all I have to say
When you do your courtin' make no display
If you want them to run after you just walk the other way
For they're mostly like the Pride of Petravore.
Chorus

*sea

The Shebeen, Dunshaughlin, Meath

Home By Bearna

This ballad originated in County Kerry, in the south-east of Ireland. It is a very popular ballad, partly I suppose because it's very easy to play - only two simple guitar chords.
Scartaglen is a village in County Kerry not far from the border with County Cork, about 5 miles from Castleisland and nine miles from Killarney. I haven't been able to find any reference to any place called Bearna in that vicinity.

Key: Am

In Scart - a - glen there lived a lass and ev - ery Sun - day af - ter Mass she would go and take a glass be - fore goin' home by Bear - na. We won't go home a - long the road for fear that you might act the rogue. Won't go home a - long the road we'll go home by Bear - na.

We won't go home across the fields, the big thornins could stick in your heels
We won't go home across the fields, we'll go home by Bearna
We won't go home around the glen, for fear your blood might rise again
We won't go home around the glen, but we'll go home by Bearna.

We won't go down the milk boreen, the night is bright we might be seen
We won't go down the milk boreen, but we'll go home by Bearna
We won't go home across the bog for fear we might meet Kearney's dog
We won't go home across the bog, but we'll go home by Bearna.

Portumna, Offaly

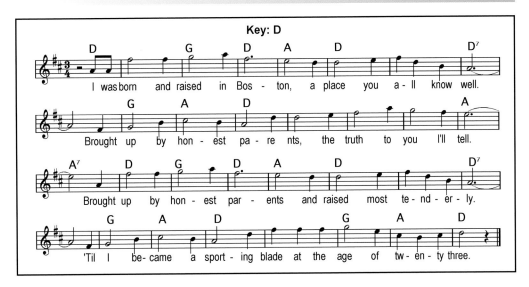

Key: D

I was born and raised in Bos - ton, a place you a - ll know well.

Brought up by hon - est pa - re nts, the truth to you I'll tell.

Brought up by hon - est par - ents and raised most te - nd - er - ly.

'Til I be- came a sport - ing blade at the age of tw - en - ty three.

My character was taken and I was sent to jail
My parents tried to bail me out but found it all in vain
The jury found me guilty the clerk he wrote it down
The judge he passed my sentence, to be sent to Charlestown.

I see my aged father and he standing by the Bar
Likewise my aged mother and she tearing at her hair
The tearing of her old grey locks and the tears came mingled down
Saying "John my son, what have you done that you're bound for Charlestown?".

There is a girl in Boston, a place you all know well
And if e'er I get my liberty it's with her I will dwell
If e'er I get my liberty bad company I will shun
The robbing of the National Bank and the drinking of the rum.

You lads that are at liberty should keep it while you can
Don't roam the streets by night or day or break the laws of man
For if you do you're sure to rue and become a lad like me
A-serving up your youthful years in the Royal Artillery.

Doolin, Clare

Dicey Riley

(Verses and chorus have the same melody)

This is a great old Dublin street ballad and I've heard many different versions of it over the years.

I'm sure that Dicey Riley (or Reilly) was a well know character in Dublin but I have no information about her.

"Heart of the rowl" is an old Dublin expression for the end of a roll of tobacco. Many years ago tobacco was sold in long lengths which were rolled up into a coil. It was commonly believed that the tail end pieces of the roll in the centre of the coil, which would be the last pieces to be sold, were more flavoursome because they would have matured the longest. Therefore the 'heart of the rowl (roll)' always signified the very best.

Fitzgibbon Street is situated on the north side of Dublin's inner city, as is the area known as Summerhill.

"Sup" and "little drop" are references to booze, which Dicey Riley was evidently very fond of!

She walks along Fitzgibbon Street with an independent air
And then it's down by Summerhill where the people stop and stare
She says "It's nearly half past one, it's time I had another little one"
Ah the heart of the rowl is Dicey Riley. *Chorus*

She owns a little sweet shop at the corner of the street
And every evening after school I go to wash her feet
She leaves me there to mind the shop while she nips in for another little drop
Ah the heart of the rowl is Dicey Riley. *Chorus*

*Old

Ballyshannon, Donegal

Poteen (Poitín)

Up to the middle of the 17th century the ordinary Irish people used to distill their own spirits and nobody bothered them.

But successive Governments, who were constantly engaged in expensive wars, started to search for new methods of taxation to fund their activities. And in 1661 a tax on spirits was introduced.

The Irish people in typical fashion completely ignored this tax and nothing was done about it for a hundred years.

In 1760 the Government thought of a better idea and passed legislation requiring all distillers to hold a licence. Some distillers complied but most didn't and therefore, overnight, the business of illicit distillation was born.

As the spirit duty was increased so also was the popularity and necessity for the illicit distiller. The authorities found it very difficult to catch them. They were protected by the community, their equipment was cheap and portable, and as long as they had an isolated spot, running water and turf they could work away without interruption.

Most of the licensed distillers were small operations. The 1782 Excise Returns confirmed that the average rural licensed distillery's output was 200-300 gallons per year.

In 1775 the duty on spirits was raised considerably thus forcing many of the smaller distilleries into the illegal arena.

In 1780 the authorities decided to impose a minimum spirit levy, forcing all distilleries to manufacture a minimum number of gallons per week regardless of whether or not they could sell it.

Shortly after that the authorities introduced new regulations insisting that distilleries 'charge their still' and manufacture product twice every week, and by 1800 this had increased to once every day.

These new regulations forced literally hundreds of small distilleries into illicit distillation.

An additional, and very important, aspect of the new regulations was that the quality of the legal product, or 'parliament whiskey', was rapidly deteriorating as distilleries were obliged to work faster and faster.

In the first decades of the 19th century sales of Poitín (as the illicit product became known) soared purely on its quality. It was more expensive than the 'parliament whiskey' and was sought after by the wealthier classes who were willing to pay for a superior product.

The Excise men and the military were charged with flushing out the poitín makers. Their rate of success was quite poor however.

Around 1787 bounty hunters were introduced and these men who normally operated in small bands had private contracts with the authorities to hunt out illicit distillers for a fee. In 1818 these bounty hunters were formed into the Revenue Police. They were armed, received regular pay plus 'bounties' and had two permanent stations - one at Ballina in County Mayo and the other at Sligo town.

In 1823 the regulations were eased to allow the licensed distillery to take more time to distil, thus improving the quality of the product. The poitín makers came under increased attack.

By 1823 poitín-making was practised extensively in the following counties: Donegal, Tyrone, Derry, Mayo, Galway, Clare, Leitrim, Antrim, Sligo and Tipperary. According to Government officials these were the 'most infected areas'.

Throughout the 1840's and the Great Famine the demand for poitín declined. The Church played an important part in curbing consumption in some areas and a vigorous campaign was initiated by Father Matthew (1790 - 1856) to curb the consumption of alcohol.

In 1857 the Revenue Police were disbanded having proved to be totally ineffective. The Royal Irish Constabulary took over responsibility for curbing the making of poitín and they enjoyed greater success.

But in spite of all the modern facilities enjoyed by our police force (Gardaí) the making of poitín still continues throughout rural Ireland.

The recipies vary from region to region. Initially poitín was made with barley or malt but today such ingredients as potatoes, treacle, beet and sugar are often used with no diminution of quality.

In 1977 a Connemara-based co-op, Comhar-chumann Cois Fharraige initiated a campaign to have poitín-making legalised and established locally as a craft industry. The Government has not yet relented.

The name 'poitín' has been patented and the campaign to have it legalised will continue for a long time to come.

In the meantime the illicit distillers show no signs of going away!

(Verses and chorus have the same melody)

This lively ballad concerns the making of poitín in the west of Ireland, and the efforts of the illicit distillers to stay one step ahead of the Excise men.

Connemara is a very picturesque area of mountain country stretching northwards from Galway city to Killary Harbour on the Atlantic and bounded to the east by Loughs Corrib and Mask.

The ballad suggests that that Excise men themselves were very fond of the poitín and this was in fact quite true.

In the early part of the 19th century, poitín was of a far higher standard than the legal 'parliament whiskey' and was much sought after, even by those who were supposed to be closing down the illicit stills!

The tradition of this ballad is that the first two lines of the last verse ('stand your ground', etc) should be sung very slowly followed by a pause, and the remainder of the verse to be speeded up immediately.

For other ballads about poitín in this book see "The Moonshiner" - page 66 and "I'm A Rover" - page 38

For more information about poitín see the opposite page.

Key: D

Gath-er up your pots and the old tin cans, the mash, the worm, the bar-ley and the bran. Run like the dev-il from the Ex-cise man. Keep the smoke from ris-ing bar - ney

Keep your eyes well peeled today
The Excise men are on their way
Searching for the mountain tay*
In the hills of Connemara.
Chorus

Swing to the left, swing to the right
The Excise men will dance all night
Drinkin' up the tay till the broad daylight
In the hills of Connemara.
Chorus

A gallon for the butcher and a quart for John
And a bottle for poor old Father Tom
To help the poor old dear along
In the hills of Connemara.
Chorus

Stand your ground, for it's too late
The Excise men are at the gate
Glory be to Paddy, but they're drinkin' it straight
In the hills of Connemara!
Repeat chorus twice

*tea

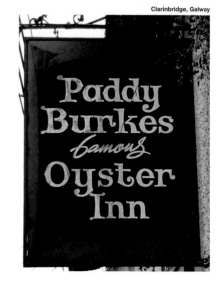

Clarinbridge, Galway

Key: D

In the sweet Coun-ty Lim-erick one cold win-ter's night, all the turf fires were burn-ing when I saw the light, and a drunk-en old mid-wife was tip-sy with joy as she danced 'round the floor with her slip of a boy, sing-ing "Ban-ye na mo is an gow - na*, and the juice of the bar-ley for me".

Well when I was a gassoon** of eight years or so
With me turf and me primer to school I did go
To a dusty old schoolhouse without any door
Where lay the schoolmaster blind drunk on the floor. *Chorus*

At the learning I wasn't such a genius I'm thinking
But I soon bet the master entirely at drinking
Not a wake nor a wedding for five miles around
But meself in the corner was sure to be found. *Chorus*

One Sunday the priest read me out from the alter
Saying "You'll end up your days with your neck in a halter
And you'll dance a fine jig betwixt heaven and hell"
And the words they did frighten, the truth for to tell. *Chorus*

So the very next morning as the dawn it did break
I went down to the vestry the pledge for to take
And there in that room sat the priests in a bunch
'Round a big roaring fire drinking tumblers of punch. *Chorus*

Well from that day to this I have wandered alone
I'm a Jack of all Trades and a master of none
With the sky for me roof and the earth for me floor
And I'll dance out me days drinking whiskey galore. *Chorus*

*Pronounced "Ban-ya na mo iss an gow-na" (The milk of the cow and the calf)
** Young lad.

Milltown, Galway

This ballad is found in England, Scotland, North America and Ireland. It is also known as "Rosin The Beau" and the first recorded printing of it was in "English Folk Songs" (1891) edited by William Barrett.

There were many ballads composed to this air in the 19th century, including "Acres Of Clams" and Lincoln And Liberty".

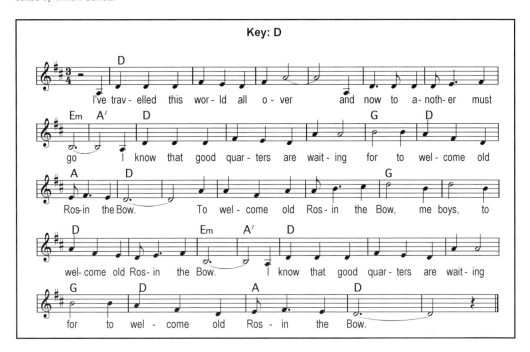

When I'm dead and laid out on the counter; a voice you will hear from below
Saying "Send down a hogshead of whiskey; to drink with old Rosin the Bow"
To drink with old Rosin the Bow, me lads; to drink with old Rosin the Bow
Saying "Send down a hogshead of whiskey; to drink with old Rosin the Bow".

And get a half dozen stout fellows; and stack them all up in a row
Let them drink out of half gallon bottles; to the memory of Rosin the Bow
To the memory of Rosin the Bow, me lads; to the memory of Rosin the Bow
Let them drink out of half gallon bottles; to the memory of Rosin the Bow.

Now get this half dozen stout fellows; and let them all stagger and go
And dig a great hole in the meadow; and in it put Rosin the Bow
And in it put Rosin the Bow, me lads; and in it put Rosin the Bow
And dig a great hole in the meadow; and in it put Rosin the Bow.

Now get ye a couple of bottles; put one at me head and me toe
With a diamond ring scratch out upon them; the name of old Rosin the Bow
The name of old Rosin the Bow, me lads; the name of old Rosin the Bow
With a diamond ring scratch out upon them; the name of old Rosin the Bow.

I feel that old Tyrant approaching; that cruel remorseless old foe
Let me lift up my glass in his honour; take a drink with old Rosin the Bow
Take a drink with old Rosin the Bow, me lads; take a drink with old Rosin the Bow
Let me lift up my glass in his honour; take a drink with old Rosin the Bow.

(Verses and chorus have the same melody)

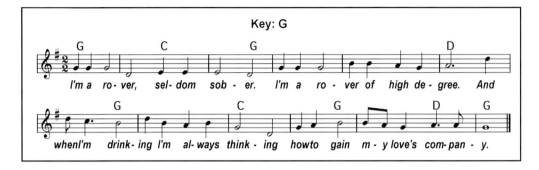

I'm a ro-ver, sel-dom sob-er. I'm a ro-ver of high de-gree. And
whenI'm drink-ing I'm al-ways think-ing howto gain m-y love's com-pan-y.

Though the night be dark as dungeon; not a star to be seen above
I will be guided without a stumble into the arms of the one I love.

He stepped up to her bedroom window kneeling gently upon a stone
And he tapped at the bedroom window; "Darling dear, do you lie alone?" ***Chorus***

"It's only me dear your own true lover; open up please and let me in
For I have travelled a weary journey and I'm near drenched to my skin".

She opened up with the greatest pleasure; unlocked the door and she let him in
They both embraced and they kissed each other; till the morning they lay as one. ***Chorus***

The cocks were waking the birds were whistling; the streams they ran free about the brae
"Remember lass I'm a ploughman's laddie and the farmer I must obey".

"Now my love I must go and leave thee and though the hills they are high above
I will climb them with greater pleasure for I've gained your undying love". ***Chorus***

Newport, Mayo

After a hard day's work, Handles Bar, Thomas Street, Dublin

The Town Of Ballybay

Ballybay is a small town set among low lying hills on the shores of Lough Major - head-water of the Dromore River, a tributary of the River Erne. It is situated in County Monaghan, an inland county in the north-east of the Irish Republic. Whether or not such a lassie ever existed in Ballybay is best left to the imagination!

"Shimmy" is an old word for night-dress or long vest.

"Courting" is a quaint Irish verb which means, in its broadest sense, to "get romantically involved with". It would cover every activity from holding hands, to gentle kissing, to a whole lot of other things! I think in this ballad the meaning is "a whole lot of other things!"

"Childer" means "children".

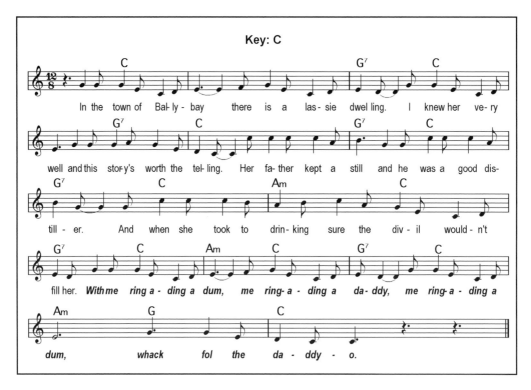

Key: C

In the town of Bal-ly-bay there is a las-sie dwel ling. I knew her ve-ry well and this story's worth the tel-ling. Her fa-ther kept a still and he was a good dis-till - er. And when she took to drin-king sure the div - il would - n't fill her. *With me ring a-ding a dum, me ring-a-ding a da-ddy, me ring-a-ding a dum, whack fol the da-ddy-o.*

She had a wooden leg that was hollow down the middle
She used to tie a string on it and play it like a fiddle
She fiddled in the hall and she fiddled in the alleyway
She didn't give a damn she had to fiddle anyway. *Chorus*

She said she couldn't dance unless she had her wellie on
But when she had it on she could dance as well as anyone
She wouldn't go to bed unless she had her shimmy on
But when she had it on she would go as quick as anyone. *Chorus*

She had lovers by the score, every Tom and Dick and Harry
She was courting night and day but still she wouldn't marry
And then she fell in love with a fella with a stammer
When he tried to run away, she hit him with a hammer. *Chorus*

She had childer up the stairs, she had childer in the brier
Another ten or twelve sitting roaring by the fire
She fed them on potatoes and on soup she made with nettles
And on lumps of hairy bacon that she boiled up in a kettle. *Chorus*

She led a sheltered life, eating porridge and black puddin'
And she terrorised her man till he up'd and died right sudden
And when the husband died she was feeling very sorry
So she rolled him in a bag and she threw him in a quarry. *Chorus*

Camden Street, Dublin

The Irish Rover

This very popular ballad was written by J.M. Crofts.

There was Barney Magee, from the banks of the Lee
There was Hogan from County Tyrone
There was Johnny McGurk, who was scared stiff of work
And a chap from Westmeath named Malone
There was Sluggler O'Toole, who was drunk as a rule
And fighting Bill Tracey from Dover
And your man Mick McCann, from the banks of the Bann
Was the skipper of the Irish Rover.

We had one million bags of the best Silgo rags
We had two million barrels of bone
We had three million bales of old nanny goats tails
We had four million barrels of stone
We had five million hogs and six million dogs
And seven million barrels of porter
We had eight million sides of old blind horses hides
In the hold of the Irish Rover.

We had sailed seven years when the measles broke out
And our ship lost her way in the fog
And the whole of the crew was reduced down to two
'Twas meself, and the captain's old dog
Then the ship struck a rock, O Lord what a shock
And nearly tumbled over
Nine times turned around, then the poor old dog was drowned
I'm the last of the Irish Rover.

Shrule, Mayo

Barry Keenan, behind the counter in his bar in Tarmonbarry, Roscommon

(The chorus melody is the same as the last two lines of the verse)

This ballad was written by Cathal McGarvey (1866 - 1927) to an old Scottish air. The oldest version of the air is in "Tea Table Miscellany", a collection of English and Scottish ballads in three volumes edited by the Scottish poet Allan Ramsay

(1686 - 1758).
The air has been used for many other ballads, including "Divers And Lazarus", "The Murder Of Maria Martin" and "Claudy Banks".

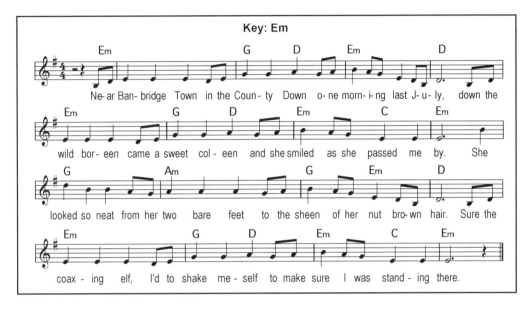

From Bantry Bay up to Derry Quay; from Galway to Dublin Town
No maid I've seen like the sweet colleen that I met in the County Down.

As she onward sped sure I shook my head and I gazed with a feeling quare
And I said, says I, to a passer-by; "whose the maid with the nut-brown hair?"
Oh he smiled at me and with pride says he; "that's the gem of Ireland's crown
She's young Rosie McCann from the banks of the Bann; she's the Star of the County Down". ***Chorus***

She'd a soft brown eye and a look so sly and a smile like a rose in June
And you craved each note from her lily-white throat as she lilted an Irish tune
At the pattern dance you'd be held in trance as she tripped through a jig or a reel
When her eyes she'd roll she would lift your soul and your heart she would quickly steal. ***Chorus***

Now I've roamed a bit but was never hit since my travelling days began
But fair and square I surrendered there to the charms of young Rosie McCann
With my heart to let sure no tenant yet did I meet with a shawl or a gown
But in she went and I asked no rent from the Star of the County Down. ***Chorus***

At the cross-roads fair I'll be surely there and I'll dress in my Sunday clothes
With me shoes all bright and me hat cocked right for a smile from the nut-brown rose
No pipe I'll smoke and no horse I'll yoke let my plough with the rust turn brown
Till a smiling bride by my own fireside be the Star of the County Down. ***Chorus***

Quare Bungle Rye

The original ballad from which the present one derives was called "The Oyster Girl" and a version is to be found in the Bodleian Library at Oxford University dating back to the 1820's.

Variants of this ballad have been found in Aberdeenshire, Somerset, Northern Ireland and North Carolina under such titles as "The Basket of Oysters", "Eggs In Her Basket" and "Quare Bungo Rye".

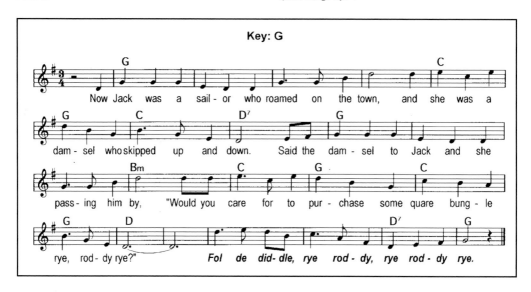

Thought Jack to himself now what can this be
But the finest of whiskey from old Germany
Smuggled up in a basket and sold on the sly
And the name that it goes by is quare bungle rye roddy rye. *Chorus*

Jack gave her a pound and he thought nothing strange
She said "hold the basket till I run for your change"
Jack looked in the basket and a baby did spy
"Begorra" says he "This is quare bungle rye roddy rye!". *Chorus*

Now to get the child christened was Jack's first intent
And to get the child christened to the parson he went
Said the parson to Jack, "What will he go by?"
"Bedad now", says Jack, "call him quare bungle rye roddy rye". *Chorus*

Now all you bold sailors who roam on the town
Beware of the damsels who skip up and down
Take a look in their baskets as they pass you by
Or else they may sell you some quare bungle rye roddy rye. *Chorus*

Ballyshannon, Donegal

Kilgarvan, Kerry

At last the shoe is on the other foot and we have a ballad about the women and 'the drink'!
This is a very popular English ballad which has successfully travelled across the Irish sea and is heard at many's a good Irish ballad session
I first came across it on the Fairport Convention album "Tipplers Tales"

Then up comes bouncing Suzy, her cheeks as red as bloom
"Move up me jolly sisters and give young Suzy room
For I will be your equal before the night is out."
These four drunken maidens, they pushed the jug about.

There's woodcock and there's pheasant, there's partridge and there's hare
There's all sorts of dainties; no scarcity was there
There's forty quarts of beer, me boys; they nearly drunk them out
These four drunken maidens, they pushed the jug about.

Then up and comes the landlord; he's asking for his pay
It's a forty shilling bill, me boys, these girls have got to pay
That's ten bob apiece, me boys, but still they wouldn't go out
These four drunken maidens, they pushed the jug about.

"Oh, where are your feathered hats, your mantles rich and fine?"
"They've all been swallowed up me boys in tankards of good wine."
"And where are your maidenheads, you maidens brisk and gay?"
"We left them in the alehouse. We drank them clean away!"

Whiskey, You're The Devil

This is a great military marching song.

A version of this was popularised by Laim Clancy and the Clancy Brothers on an album in 1955 entitled "The Lark in the Morning"

There was also another version of the song, similar to this one, which went under the title "Johnny and Molly".

This ballad was published in the collection "Six Hundred and Seventeen Irish Ballads" (c. 1900).

The song also appears in "The British Soldier" by J.H. Stocqueler (1857), although without any chorus.

Lewis Winstock in his book "Songs and Music of the Redcoats" states that this song 'was particularly popular with the 88th Connaught Rangers, and a regiment nicknamed The Black Belts sang it as they left Dublin in 1809 for the fever-ridden swamps of Walcheren'.

Whiskey, you're the devil, you're leading me astray
Over hills and mountain and to Americay
You're sweeter, stronger, decenter, your spunkier than tay*
Oh whiskey, you're my darling, drunk or sober.

Come on brave boys we're on for marching
First for France and then for Spain
While canons roar and men are dying
March brave boys there's no denying
Love, fare you well
Chorus

I think I hear the Colonel crying
"March, brave boys there's no denying
Colours flying, drums a-beating
March brave boys there's no retreating"
Love, fare you well
Chorus

The mother cries "Oh do not wrong me
Do not take my daughter from me
For if you do I will torment you
And after death my ghost will haunt you"
Love, fare you well
Chorus

Molly dear do not grieve for me
I'm off to fight for Ireland's glory
If we live we'll be victorious
If we die our souls are glorious
Love, fare you well

Chorus

*tea

Near Donadea, Kildare. No, it's not your eyesight, nor my camera.
Roches is actually slowly sinking into the surrounding bog!

Johnny Jump Up

(Verse and chorus have the same melody)

Rumour has it that this song, based on an old traditional Irish air, was written by Tim (Tadhg) Jordan of Cork City.
Johnny Jump Up was the slang name given to a particular type of cider.
In years gone by when there was a shortage of materials cider was sometimes stored in whiskey casks. The cider absorbed the spirit from the wood and the resultant beverage was very potent and had a kick like a mule!
It became known as 'Johnny Jump Up'.
The reference to the 'Lee Road' is a reference to the Mental Hospital which is located there.

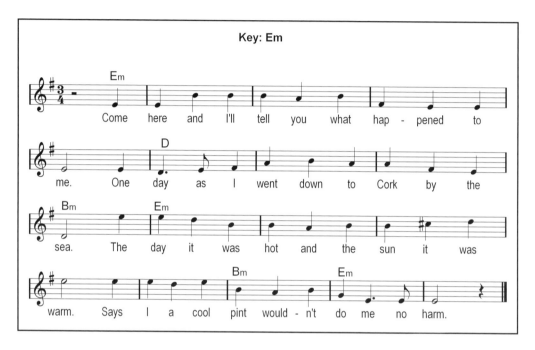

Key: Em

Come here and I'll tell you what hap - pened to
me. One day as I went down to Cork by the
sea. The day it was hot and the sun it was
warm. Says I a cool pint would - n't do me no harm.

Oh never, oh never, oh never again
If I live to a hundred or a hundred-and-ten
I fell to the ground and I couldn't get up
After drinking a sup of that Johnny Jump Up

I went in and I called for a bottle of stout
Says the barman, I'm sorry, all the beer is sold out
Try whiskey or paddy, ten years in the wood
Says I, I'll try cider, I've heard that it's good
After downing the third I went out to the yard
Where I bumped into Brody, the big civic guard
Come here to me boy, don't you know I'm the law?
Well, I uped with me fist and I shattered his jaw.
Chorus

Ennistymon, Clare

He fell to the ground with his knees doubled up
But it wasn't I hit him, 'twas Johnny Jump Up
Next thing I remember down in Cork by the sea
Was a cripple on crutches and says he to me
"I'm afraid of me life I'll be hit by a car
Won't you help me across to the Celtic Knot Bar?"
After drinking a quart of that cider so sweet
He threw down his crutches and danced on his feet.
Chorus

I went down the Lee Road, a friend for to see
They call it the madhouse in Cork by the sea
Well when I got there, sure the truth I will tell
They had this poor bugger locked up in a cell
Said the guard, testing him, "Say these words if you can
'Around the rugged rock the ragged rascal ran'"
Tell him I'm not crazy, tell him I'm not mad
It was only a sip of the bottle I had.
Chorus

A man died in the Lee by the name of McNabb
They washed him and laid him outside on the slab
Well after the peelers their notes they did take
His wife brought him home to a bloody fine wake
'Twas about 12 o'clock and the beer it was high
The corpse he sat up and says he with a sigh
I can't get to heaven, they won't let me up
'Til I bring them a quart of the Johnny Jump Up
Chorus

So if ever you go down to Cork by the sea
Stay out of the ale house and take it from me
If you want to stay sane don't you dare take a sup
Of that devil drink cider called Johnny Jump Up!
Chorus

Camden Street, Dublin

For Reilly played on the big bass drum
Reilly had a mind for murder and slaughter
Reilly had one big red glittering eye
And he kept that eye on his lovely daughter. *Chorus*

Her hair was black and her eyes were blue
The colonel and the major and the captain sought her
The sergeant and the private and the drummer boy too
But they never had a chance with aul' Reilly's daughter. *Chorus*

I got me a ring and a parson too
I got me a scratch in the married quarter
Settled me down to a peaceful life
As happy as a king with Reilly's daughter. *Chorus*

I hear a sudden footstep on the stair
It's the one-eyed Reilly and he lookin' for slaughter
With two pistols in his hand
Searching for the man who had married his daughter. *Chorus*

I took auld Reilly by the hair
Rammed his head into a bucket of water
Fired his pistols in the air
A damned sight quicker than I married his daughter. *Chorus*

Milltown, Galway

This page and opposite: Sixmilebridge, Clare

(Verses and chorus have the same melody)

"Courting" is a quaint Irish verb which means, in its broadest sense, to "get romantically involved with". It would cover every activity from holding hands, to gentle kissing, to a whole lot of other things!

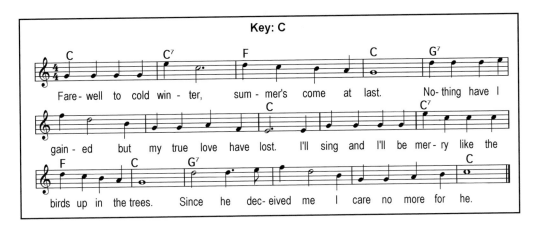

Key: C

Fare- well to cold win - ter, sum - mer's come at last. No- thing have I gain - ed but my true love have lost. I'll sing and I'll be mer - ry like the birds up in the trees. Since he dec- eived me I care no more for he.

Let him go, let him tarry, let him sink or let him swim
He doesn't care for me nor I don't care for him
He can go and get another that I hope he will enjoy
For I'm going to marry a far nicer boy.

He wrote me a letter saying he was very bad
I sent him back an answer saying I was awful glad
He wrote me another saying he was well and strong
But I care no more for him than the ground he walks upon. *Chorus*

Some of his friends they have a good kind wish for me
Others of his friends sure they could hang me on a tree
But soon I'll let them see my love and soon I'll let them know
That I can get a new sweetheart at any place I go. *Chorus*

He can go to his old mother now and set her mind at ease
I hear she's an old woman and very hard to please
It's slighting me and talking ill is what she's always done
Because I was courting her great big ugly son. *Chorus*

The Waxie's Dargle

The air of this popular Dublin ballad is a well known and recognised melody entitled "The Girl I left Behind Me" and was first published in Dublin in 1791. A traditional fife tune, it was a very popular patriotic song during the American Revolution.

In Dublin the 'Waxies' were the people who waxed bootlaces. The term was also used for candlemakers. In any event, they were without doubt members of the 'working classes' on the lower rungs of the social ladder in Dublin.

At the turn of the century in Dublin it was the practice for well-to-do folk to take summer breaks in the fashionable seaside town of Bray in County Wicklow, about 20 miles south of Dublin city. Bray was a very popular town for wealthy Dubliners and a river ran near the town called the Dargle.

Once every year the Waxies held an annual outing. They couldn't afford to go all the way the Bray so they used to go to Sandymount Strand, an extensive beach on the south side of Dublin. Sandymount Strand became known as 'The Waxie's Dargle' as it was their equivalent of the fashionable seaside resort of Bray.

In this ballad, two Dublin women are contemplating a visit to the 'Waxie's Dargle' but don't have the necessary money. "Monto Town" is a reference to the red-light district around Montgomery Street in the heart of Dublin. See "Monto" - page 14.

"Galway Races" is an annual racing festival held in Galway each year. See "The Galway Races" - page 16.

"Capel Street" is a Dublin street on the north side of the River Liffey renowned for its pawnbroking shops. In the second verse of the ballad one of the women hopes to pawn her husband's trouser braces and travel to the Galway races with the proceeds.

In some versions of the ballad 'young Kill McArdle' is replaced by 'Uncle McArdle'.

Says my oul' one to your oul' one "Will ye come to the Galway Races?"
Says your oul' one to my oul' one "With the price of me oul' lad's braces
I went down to Capel Street to the Jewman moneylender
But they wouldn't give me a couple of bob for me oul' lad's new suspenders". *Chorus*

Says my oul' one to your oul' one "We have no beef or mutton"
But if we go down to Monto town we might get a drink for nothin'
Here's a piece of advice for you which I got from an oul' fishmonger
When food is scarce and you see the hearse you'll know you died of hunger". *Chorus*

Capel Street, Dublin. One of the last surviving pawnbrokers

The Spanish Lady

This is one of my favourite ballads in the book but unfortunately I have no knowledge of its history.
Stoneybatter is a district situated on Dublin's northside. Patrick's Close and the Gloucester Diamond are areas located in Dublin city centre.

"Napper Tandy" refers to James Napper Tandy (c. 1737 - 1803) who was a prominent member of the United Irishmen and was involved in the 1798 Rising. He lived in Dublin city centre. He was captured in Hamburg, returned to Ireland and sentenced to death, but was deported to France in 1803.

Key: G

As I rode down through Dub-lin c-i-ty at the hour of twelve at night,
who should I see but a Span-ish l-a-dy wash-ing her feet by can-dle-light.
First she washed them then she dried them o-ver a fire of am-ber coal. In
all my life I ne'er did see a-a maid so sweet a-bout the soul.
Whack fol the toor-a-loor-a la-ad-ie whack fol the toor-a-loor-a lay.
Whack fol the toor-a-loor-a la-ad-ie whack fol the toor-a-loor-a lay.

As I came back through Dublin city at the hour of half past eight
Who should I spy but the Spanish Lady brushing her hair in the broad daylight
First she tossed it then she brushed it; on her lap was a silver comb
In all my life I ne'er did see a maid so fair since I did roam. ***Chorus***

As I went back through Dublin city as the sun began to set
Who should I spy but the Spanish Lady catching a moth in a golden net
When she saw me then she fled me, lifting her petticoat over her knee
In all my life I ne'er did see a maid so shy as the Spanish Lady. ***Chorus***

I wandered north and I wandered south through Stoneybatter and Patrick's Close
Up and around by the Gloucester Diamond and back by Napper Tandy's house
Old age has laid her hand upon me, cold as a fire of ashy coals
In all my life I ne'er did see a maid so sweet as the Spanish Lady. ***Chorus***

Donegal Town

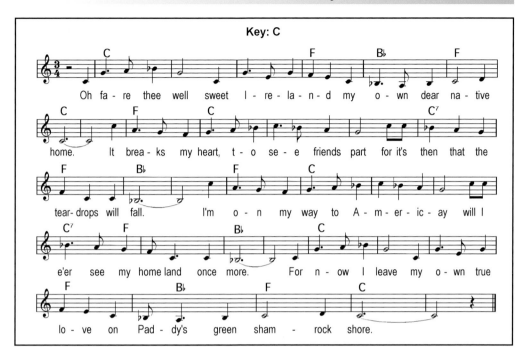

Our ship she lies at anchor now; she's standing by the quay
May fortune bright shine down each night as we sail all across the sea
Many ships have been lost, many lives it has cost on the journey that lies before
With a tear in my eye I'm bidding goodbye to Paddy's green shamrock shore.

From Londonderry we did set sail; it being the fourth of May
On a sturdy ship to cover the trip across to Americay
Fresh water then did we take in; one hundred barrels or more
For fear we'd be short before reaching port far from the shamrock shore.

Two of our anchors we did weigh before we left the quay
All down the river we were towed till we came to the open sea
We saw that night the grandest sight we ever saw before
The sun going down 'tween sea and sky far from Paddy's green shamrock shore.

Early next morn, sea-sick and forlorn, not one of us was free
And I myself was confined to bed with no one to pity me
No father or mother or sister or brother to raise my head when sore
That made me think of the family I left back on Paddy's green shamrock shore.

So fare thee well my own true love I think of you night and day
A place in my mind you surely will find although I'm so far away
Though I am alone and away from my home I'll think of the good time before
Until the day I can make my way back to Paddy's green shamrock shore.

Muirsheen Durkin

(Verses and chorus have the same melody)

This is an emigration ballad written to the melody of the Irish air "Cailiní Deas Mhuigheo" (The Beautiful Girls of Mayo"), though presented in a somewhat light-hearted manner. Instead of bemoaning the fact that he has to leave Ireland the singer is quite looking forward to making his fortune in "far Americay". Indeed, many Irish emigrants did just that over the centuries!

It is estimated that at least 8 million Irish men and women emigrated from Ireland between 1801 and 1921 and many more left during the depression years of the 20th century. The statement therefore by President Mary Robinson in December 1990, that there are at least 70 million people throughout the world who claim to be of Irish descent, is not an exaggeration.

The most common destination for Irish emigrants prior to the 1860's was Canada; between then and the First World War it was the U.S.A., and from then on it was Great Britain.

"Courting" is a quaint Irish term which means, in its broadest sense, to "get romantically involved with". It would cover every activity from holding hands, to gentle kissing, to a whole lot of other things!

Obviously the singer in this ballad spent some time in the south of Ireland, as the towns of Blarney, Kanturk, Killarney, Passage and Cobh (formerly Queenstown) are all located in the counties of Cork and Kerry. It looks as if he was a busy man down there!

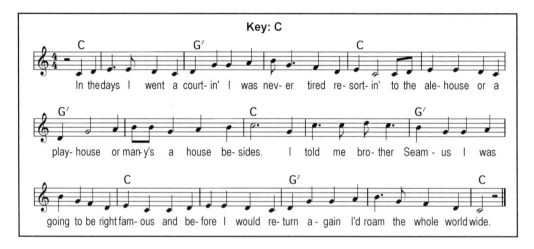

Key: C

In the days I went a courtin' I was never tired resortin' to the ale-house or a play-house or many's a house besides. I told me brother Seamus I was going to be right famous and before I would return again I'd roam the whole world wide.

Goodbye Muirsheen Durkin, sure I'm sick and tired of workin'
No more I'll dig the praties, no longer I'll be fooled
For sure's me name is Carney I'll be off to Californee
And instead of digging praties I'll be digging lumps of gold.

I've courted girls in Blarney, in Kanturk and in Killarney
In Passage and in Queenstown; that is the Cobh of Cork
But goodbye to all this pleasure sure I'm off to seek me leisure
And the next time you will hear from me is a letter from New York. ***Chorus***

So goodbye all ye boys at home I'm sailing far across the foam
I'm going to make me fortune in far Americay
There's gold and money plenty for the poor and for the gentry
And when I do return again I never more will stray. ***Chorus***

Achill Island, Mayo

THE
VALLEY HOUSE
BAR
GUINNESS

(The chorus melody is the same as the first four lines of the verse)

This very popular song was written by Percy French in the 1880's while working as a Civil Engineer in County Cavan.

It is based on a real-life character who lived in County Leitrim.

While travelling around that part of the country French used to stay with his friend, Rev. James Godley at his rectory at Carrigallen, Leitrim.

French, in his own writings tells the following tale:

"One evening the Rev. James Godley came in after one of his long walks and told me how he had met the local flute player and how he had paid his rent

'I've paid up all me arrears, yer riverence', said Phil the Fluter - for, as my readers have already surmised, 'twas himself that was in it.

'And how did you manage that?' said his reverence.

'I give a ball', said Phil.

'A ball!' said his reverence. 'If my family asked me to give a ball, I'd have to put my hand in my pocket, and I think I'd keep it there,' he added thoughtfully.

'Well', said Phil. 'You'd make a hole in a couple o' pound givin' your ball, for you'd have a young lady to play the pianna and cake and sandwidges, an' other combustibles. Now when I give a ball, I clean out me cabin and lock up any food or drink in the cupboard. Then I put me hat behind the door; the neighbours come in bringin' their suppers wid them, and each puttin' a shillin' or two in the hat. Then I cock me leg over the dresser, throw me top lip over the flute and toother away like a hatful o' larks and there they stay leppin' like hares till two in the mornin'.'"

You can now see where French got his inspiration for this song! There is further information about Percy French at the front of this book.

With the toot of the flute, and the twiddle of the fiddle, O
Hopping in the middle, like a herrin' on the griddle, O
Up, down, hands around, crossing to the wall
Oh hadn't we the gaeity at Phil the Fluther's Ball

There was Mister Denis Dogherty, who kept a runnin' dog
There was little crooked Paddy, from the Tiraloughett bog
There was boys from every barony and girls from ev'ry "art"
And the beautiful Miss Brady in a private ass and cart
And along with them came bouncing Mrs. Cafferty
Little Micky Mulligan was also to the fore
Rose, Suzanne, and Margaret O'Rafferty
The flower of Ardmagullion and the pride of Petravore
Chorus

First little Micky Mulligan got up to show them how
And then the Widda' Cafferty steps out and makes her bow
I could dance you off your legs sez she as sure as you are born
If ye'll only make the piper play "The hare was in the corn"
So Phil plays up to the best of his ability
The lady and the gentleman begin to do their share
Faith, then Mick, it's you that has agility
Begorra Mrs. Cafferty, yer leppin' like a hare!
Chorus

Then Phil the Fluther tipped a wink to little Crooked Pat
"I think it's nearly time," sez he, "for passin' round the hat"
So Paddy pass'd the caubeen round, and looking mighty cute
Sez, "Ye've got to pay the piper when he toothers on the flute"
Then all joined in with the greatest joviality
Covering the buckle and the shuffle and the cut
Jigs were danced of the very finest quality
But the Widda' bet the company at "handling the foot"
Chorus

Tullaghan, Leitrim

The Moonshiner

(Verses and chorus have the same melody)

This pleasant ballad is about that most popular of Irish alcoholic beverages, 'Poitín' or 'Poteen'. - also the subject of the ballads "Let the Grasses Grow" (page 9) and "The Hills Of Connemara" (page 35).

There are many other ballads dedicated to the pastime of making and drinking this illicit libation and of avoiding the local constabulary and Excise men in the process. All the ballads I know are in praise of this activity!

Poitín was particularly popular in rural areas and the ballad mentions Galway, a county on the West coast of Ireland. Rumour has it that poitín was (and probably still is!) extensively distilled in the Galway area.

The counties of Donegal, Sligo and Leitrim are also on the west and north-west coasts of Ireland.

There is further information on poitín to be found on page 34.

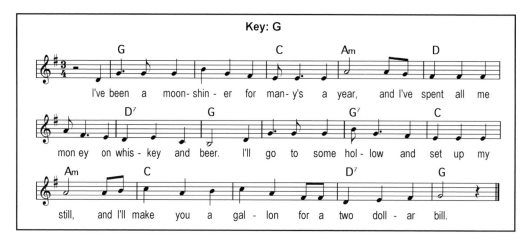

I'm a rambler, I'm a gambler, I'm a long way from home
And if you don't like me then leave me alone
I'll eat when I'm hungry, I'll drink when I'm dry
And if the moonshine don't kill me I'll live till I die.

I'll go to some hollow in this country
Ten gallons of wash and I'll go on a spree
No woman to follow and the world is all mine
I love none so well as I love the moonshine. *Chorus*

Moonshine, dear moonshine, oh how I love thee
You killed my poor father but dare you try me
Bless all the moonshiners and bless the moonshine
Its breath smells as sweet as the dew on the vine. *Chorus*

There's moonshine for Molly and moonshine for May
Moonshine for Tom and he'll sing all the day
Moonshine for me breakfast, moonshine for me tea
Moonshine oh me hearties! It's moonshine for me! *Chorus*

Belturbet, Cavan

This ballad was printed in "The Complete Collection Of Irish Music As Noted By George Petrie", published in 1903.
'Punch' is a mulled drink made up of a concoction of ingredients, but mainly alcohol. There can be several varieties of alcoholic drink mixed into the formula which can differ according to the tastes of its maker.

Naturally punch can be very potent! Because of its sweet taste and mulled properties there is a tendency to drink it quickly and in large amounts. Before you know where you are it can creep up on you and give you one hell of a wallop - hence the name! You've been warned - watch out!

What more diversion can a man desire than to sit him down by a snug coal fire
And upon his knee have a pretty wench and upon his table a jug of punch. ***Chorus***

If I was sickly and very bad and was not able for to go or stand
I would not think it at all amiss for to pledge my shoes for a jug of punch. ***Chorus***

The doctor fails with all his art to cure an impression on the heart
If life was gone but within an inch, what would bring it back but a jug of punch. ***Chorus***

But when I'm dead and within my grave no costly tombstone will I have
They'll dig a grave both wide and deep with a jug of punch at my head and feet. ***Chorus***

Mac's Bar, Bunratty Folk Park, Clare

Greenan, Wicklow

This is an old ballad with many variations in Scotland, England and Ireland. Versions have been found back as far as 1720 under titles such as "Lady Cassillis Lilt", "Johnny Faa" and "The Gypsy Laddie". The earliest known printing of it was in "Tea Table Miscellany", a collection of English and Scottish ballads in three volumes edited by the Scottish poet Allan Ramsay (1686 - 1758).

In the late 18th century this ballad was associated with John, the sixth Earl of Cassilis and his first wife Lady Jean Hamilton. Before her marriage to the Earl in the early 1600's, Jean Hamilton was in love with a gypsy, Johnny Faa of Dunbar. In later years when the Earl and Lady Jean had settled into normal domestic life, Johnny Faa returned and persuaded her to elope. Johnny Faa was hanged for this indiscretion in 1624 and Lady Jean was banished for life to a tower constructed specifically for her imprisonment. You didn't mess around in those days!

They sang sweet and they sang low and fast her tears began to flow
She laid down her silken gown her golden rings and all her show.

It was upstairs and downstairs the lady went; put on her suit of leather-o
And it was the cry all around the door "She's away with the raggle-taggle gypsy-o".

It was late that night when the lord came home enquiring for his lady-o
The servant's voice rang around the house; "She is gone with the raggle-taggle gypsy-o".

"Oh then saddle for me, my milk white steed; the black horse is not speedy-o
And I will ride and I'll seek me bride whose away with the raggle-taggle gypsy-o".

Oh then he rode high and he rode low; he rode north and south also
But when he came to a wide open field it is there that he spotted his lady-o.

"Oh then why did you leave your house and your land; why did you leave your money-o
And why did you leave your newly wedded lord to be off with the raggle-taggle gypsy-o".

"Yerra what do I care for me house and me land and what do I care for money-o
And what do I care for my newly-wedded lord; I'm away with the raggle-taggle gypsy-o".

"And what do I care for my goose-feathered bed with blankets drawn so comely-o
Tonight I'll sleep in the wide open field all along with the raggle-taggle gypsy-o".

"Oh for you rode east when I rode west; you rode high and I rode low
I'd rather have a kiss from the yellow gypsy's lips than all your land and money-o".

The Jolly Beggarman

The air of this old ballad is thought to have originated in Scotland, the 'Jolly Beggarman' being King James V of Scotland. James V (1513 - 1545) had a reputation for wandering around in the disguise of a vagrant and chasing innocent unsuspecting maidens.

The lyrics first appeared in print in the 1730's in England.

Key: C

It's of a jol-ly beg-gar-man came trip-ping o'er the plai-ns. He came un-to a far-mer's door a lodg-ing for to ga-in. The far-mer's daugh-ter she came down and viewed him cheek and ch-in. She said "He is a hand-some man I pray you take him i-n". *We'll go no more a-ro-ov-ing, a-rov-ing in the ni-gh-t, we'll go no more a-rov-ing let the mo-on shine so br-igh-t. We'll go no more a-rov-ing.*

He would not lie within the barn nor yet within the byre
But he would in the corner lie down by the kitchen fire
And then the beggar's bed was made of good clean sheets and hay
And down beside the kitchen fire the jolly beggar lay. *Chorus*

The farmer's daughter she got up to bolt the kitchen door
And there she saw the beggar standing naked on the floor
He took the daughter in his arms and to the bed he ran
"Kind sir", she said "Be easy now, you'll waken our good man". *Chorus*

"O no, you are no beggar man, you are some gentleman
For you have stole my maidenhead and I am quite undone"
"I am no lord, I am no squire, of beggars I be one
And beggars they be robbers all and you are quite undone". *Chorus*

The farmer's wife came down the stairs, awakened from her sleep
She saw the beggar and the girl and she began to weep
She took the bed in both her hands and threw it at the wall
Saying "Go you with the beggar man, your maidenhead and all!". *Chorus*

'The North Pole' bar, Dumphries, Co Donegal

Anascaul, Kerry.
'The South Pole Inn' was owned and operated by the legendary Antartic explorer Tom Crean between 1927 and 1938

The Parting Glass

This is a great song to wind up an evening and many's a balladeer uses it as the closing song to a session. It is well known in both Ireland and Scotland.

It was printed on broadsides as early as 1770 - many of these can be found in the Bodleian Library. It was also published in the song collection "Scots Musical Museum" (1803).

The melody appears in the Skene and Guthrie Manuscripts of the 17th century.

There is normally a lengthy pause at the end of each line.

If you saw the hilarious film "Waking Ned Devine" (set in a rural town in Ireland but actually shot in the Isle of Man) you would have heard this song being performed as the credits rolled at the end.

Of all the comrades ever I had, they're sorry for my going away
And all the sweethearts ever I had, they wished me one more day to stay
But since it falls unto my lot that I should rise and you should not
I gently rise and softly call, good night and joy be with you all.

If I had money enough to spend and leisure time to sit a while
There is a fair maid in this town that sorely has my heart beguiled
Her rosy cheeks and ruby lips, by own she has my heart enthralled
Then fill to me the parting glass, good night and joy be with you all.

'The Tin Pub', Ahakista, Cork

A drop o' the pure!

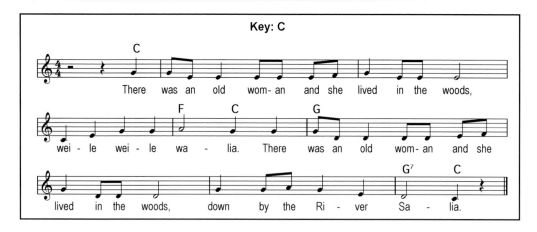

She had a baby three months old, weile, weile, walia
She had a baby three months old, down by the River Salia.

She had a pen-knife long and sharp, weile, weile, walia
She had a pen-knife long and sharp, down by the River Salia.

She stuck the pen-knife in the baby's heart, weile, weile, walia
She stuck the pen-knife in the baby's heart, down by the River Salia.

Three loud knocks came a-knocking on the door, weile, weile, walia
Three loud knocks came a-knocking on the door, down by the River Salia.

Two policemen and a man, weile, weile, walia
Two policemen and a man, down by the River Salia.

"Are you the woman that killed the child", weile, weile, walia
"Are you the woman that killed the child", down by the River Salia.

They tied her hands behind her back, weile, weile, walia
They tied her hands behind her back, down by the River Salia.

The rope was pulled and she got hung, weile, weile walia
The rope was pulled and she got hung, down by the River Salia.

And that was the end of the woman in the woods, weile, weile, walia
And that was the end of the baby too, down by the River Salia.

Grange, Sligo

The Shores Of Americay

This is a ballad about emigration.

Most Irishmen and women emigrated because of necessity. However the writer of this ballad is not leaving because of economic necessity, but rather to carve out a new life for his beloved and himself in America.

The sentiments in this ballad are not unlike those expressed in "Muirsheen Durkin" (page 62).

It is estimated that at least 8 million Irish men and women emigrated from Ireland between 1801 and 1921 and many more left during the depression years of the 20th century. The statement, therefore, by President Mary Robinson in December 1990, that there are at least 70 million people throughout the world who claim to be of Irish descent, is not an exaggeration.

The most common destination for Irish emigrants prior to the 1860's was Canada; between then and the First World War it was the U.S.A., and from then on it was Great Britain.

Key: C

I'm bid-ding fare-well to the land of my youth and the home that I love so well, and the moun-tains so grand in my own nat-ive land I'm bid ding them a-ll fare-well. With an a-ch-ing heart I will bid them a-dieu, to-mor-row I sail far a-way. O'er the r-ag-ing foam for to seek out a home on the shores of Am-er-ic-ay.

And it's not for the want of employment I go, and it's not for the love of fame
Or that fortune so bright may shine over me and give me a glorious name
No it's not for the want of employment I go o'er the stormy and perilous sea
But to seek a new home for my own true love on the shores of Americay.

And when I am bidding my final farewell the teardrops like rain will blind
To think of my friends in my own native land and the home that I'm leaving behind
And If I'm to die in a foreign land and be buried so distant away
No fond mother's tears will be shed o'er my grave on the shores of Americay.

In the village of Horse & Jockey, Tipperary

I've come across this ballad in various different forms both in Ireland and England. The oldest printed version is called "Old Woman From Blighter Town" but there are also versions in England where the old woman is from Yorkshire or Dover. There is a version entitled "Tipping It Up To Nancy" (page 79) recorded by the Irish folk singer Christy Moore on his first album "Paddy on the Road" in 1969.

I've never tried eating 'eggs and marrowbones' so I couldn't tell you whether or not the potion works!

County Wexford is in the south-eastern corner of Ireland with a long coastline on both the Irish Sea and the Celtic Sea. On the north it is bounded by the hill of County Wicklow and on the west by the River Barrow and the Blackstairs Mountains. Wexford played host to King Henry II in 1172 when he came over from England to Selskar Abbey to do penance for the murder of Thomas á Becket. It is also well-known as the birthplace of the family of the former American President, John F. Kennedy.

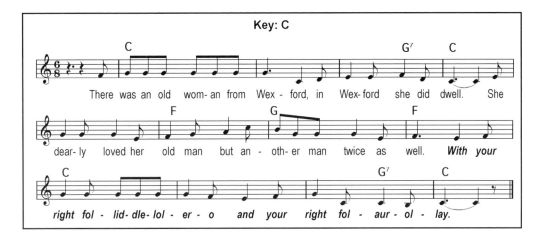

One day she went to the doctor for some medicine for to find
Says she "Will ye give me something for to make me old man blind". *Chorus*

"Feed him eggs and marrowbones and make him suck them all
And it won't be very long before he won't see you at all". *Chorus*

The doctor wrote a letter and he signed it with his hand
And he sent it to the old man so that he would understand. *Chorus*

She fed him eggs and marrowbones and made him suck them all
And it wasn't very long before he couldn't see the wall. *Chorus*

Said he "I'd like to drown myself but that would be a sin"
Said she "I'll come along with you and help to push you in". *Chorus*

The woman she stepped back a bit to rush and push him in
But the old man quickly stepped aside and she went tumbling in. *Chorus*

How loudly she did holler oh how loudly she did call
"Yerra hold your whist old woman sure I can't see you at all". *Chorus*

Now eggs and eggs and marrowbones may make your old man blind
But if you want to drown him you must creep up from behind. *Chorus*

(Verses and chorus have the same melody)

This very popular ballad was recorded some years ago by the Irish folk group, The Dubliners.

In the song the singer is lamenting the fact that he has spent all of his money on the three pastimes much favoured by many's an Irishman - Wine, Women and Song (or, as some cruder folk would have it - 'Booze, Birds and Ballads').

There are other versions of this ballad - "My Jolly Jolly Tar" (1904) and "The Nobby Hat" (1906). The ballad is also know as "Here's To The Grog".

'Grog' was a mixture of rum and water but the name gradually became a term for alcohol in general.

Grog was served as a ration in the United States Navy until 1862, and in the British Navy until 1970.

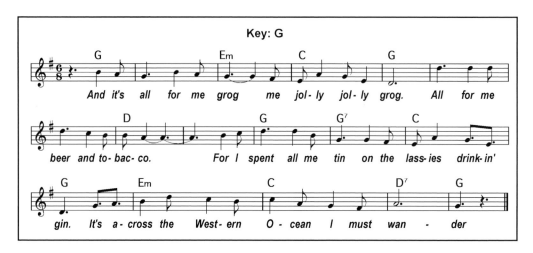

Where are me boots, me noggin' noggin' boots
They're all gone for beer and tobacco
For the heels are worn out and the toes are kicked about
And the soles are lookin' out for better weather. ***Chorus***

Where is me shirt, me noggin' noggin' shirt
It's all gone for beer and tobacco
For the collar is all worn and the sleeves they are all torn
And the tail is lookin' out for better weather. ***Chorus***

I'm sick in the head and I haven't been to bed
Since I first came ashore from me slumber
For I spent all me dough on the lassies, don't you know
Far across the Western Ocean I must wander. ***Chorus***

Athlone, Westmeath

See "The Old Woman From Wexford" - page 77 for another completely different version of this song.

Key: D

There was a wom-an in o - ur town, a wom-an you all know
well. She dear - ly loved her hus - band but an - oth-er man twice as
we - ll. **With me right finn- ick- an - air - ee - o, me tip finn- ick a
wall, with me right finn- ick - an - air - ee - o, we're tipp- in' it up to Nan - cy.**

She went down to the chemist shop some remedies for to find
"Have you anything in your chemist shop to make me old man blind?" **Chorus**

"Give him eggs and marrowbones and make him suck them all
And before he has the last one sucked he won't see you at all". **Chorus**

She gave him eggs and marrowbones and made him suck them all
Before he had the last one sucked he couldn't see the wall. **Chorus**

"If in this world I cannot see, then here I cannot stay
"I'd rather go and drown meself"; says she "I'll show the way". **Chorus**

She led him to the river and she led him to the brim
But sly enough of the old lad it was him that shoved her in. **Chorus**

"Oh husband dear I'm going to drown don't leave me here behind!"
"Yerra shut your mouth" the old lad said, "sure don't ye know I'm blind". **Chorus**

Lisdoonvarna, Clare.
Home to the annual
International Bachelor's
Festival

The Holy Ground

This is a great Irish ballad of the sea, or 'shanty', made famous and popular by a rousing recording of it by The Clancy Brothers. There are two other ballads I've heard of set to the same tune - "Old Swansea Town Once More" and "The Lass of Swansea Town".

This ballad is set in the town of Cobh, a fishing village located in Cork Harbour about 8 miles east of Cork city

Cobh was the embarkation point for many Irish men and women emigrating to America

During the period of the Napoleonic Wars (1792 - 1815) Cork Harbour grew in importance as a refuelling and assembly point for naval and commercial shipping. Today Cobh is still the principal Irish port-of-call for transatlantic liners. In 1838 a steamer called "Sirius" left the port of Cobh and became the first to cross the Atlantic, taking 18 days.

On April 11th 1912 the Titanic called into Cobh on her maiden voyage.

The name of Cobh was changed to 'Queenstown' in 1849 to commemorate a visit to Ireland by Queen Victoria but the former name was readopted in 1922.

The name 'The Holy Ground' is given to that part of the town situated on the east side (although there are also suggestions that the Hold Ground was a renowned brothel in the town, but I can't get anybody to confirm this!).

When in Cobh you should visit the "Cobh - The Queenstown Story" Visitor Centre, a multimedia exhibition on the origins, history and legacy of Cobh.

A sea shanty is a song sung by sailors while carrying out their tasks at sea. They have distinct and separate rhythms for the various chores performed at sea. Many of the shanties involved a principle singer and a choral response and they served both as a mental diversion and as an aid to synchronised teamwork. Some shanties also provided an outlet for sailors to voice their opinions without the risk of punishment! The main types of shanties were (1) Capstan Shanties, sung by sailors as they marched around the capstan to raise the anchor, (2) Halyard Shanties, sung by sailors as they raised and lowered the sails. This could be very heavy work and usually the crew would rest during the verse and haul during the chorus, (3) Short Drag Shanties, sung by sailors during heavy duty work, (4) Windlass and Pumping Shanties. The windlass was a pumping apparatus used on some ships to raise the anchor. Manual water pumps were also fitted to most ships. These types of shanty were sung to the rhythm of the pump action.

If you're heading off on a sea journey somewhere there's no need for you to learn a bunch of sea shanties. They tell me that computers and electronic gadgets now do all of the work!

For more information on sea shanties, check out the internet site "www.shanty.org".

And now the storm is raging and we are far from the shore
And the night is dark and dreary and our happy thoughts no more
And the good ship she is tossed about and the rigging is all torn
But still I live in hope to see the Holy Ground once more, FINE GIRL YOU ARE! *Chorus*

And now the storm is over and we are safe and well
We will go into a public house and we'll eat and drink our fill
And we'll drink strong ale and porter and make the rafters roar
And when our money is all spent we'll go to sea once more, FINE GIRL YOU ARE! *Chorus*

Parnell Square, Dublin

There are many versions of this popular ballad to be found in Ireland and Britain. One version, with many similarities to this one, was first printed in 1636 and was to be sung to the tune "If 'Be The Dad On't". A later version, entitled "The Old Maid's Last Prayer" was printed around 1825. Another similar ballad entitled "The Poor Auld Maid" was published in 'Folk Songs Of The North-East' (1914).

You'd have to pity the poor unfortunate Annie in the ballad. Nowadays there are singles bars, singles clubs and all sorts of opportunities for women to pursue and ensnare (did I say that?) unsuspecting and innocent men. Indeed a popular and internationally renowned Matchmaking Festival takes place every October in the town of Lisdoonvarna, County Clare.

The Lisdoonvarna Matchmaking Festival is now gaining a reputation in the USA as the best opportunity for a woman to meet up with a real home-grown Irishman with a view to friendship, marriage, etc.

Key: G

I have of-ten heard it said by my fath-er and my moth-er that going to a wed-ding was the mak-ings of an-oth-er. Well if this be so then I'll go with-out a bid-ding. Oh it's kind Prov-id-ence, won't you send me to a wed-ding! *For it's oh de-ar me, how will it be if I die an old maid in the gar - ret!*

Oh now there's my sister Jean; she's not handsome nor good-looking
Scarcely sixteen and a fella she was courting
Now she's twenty-four with a son and a daughter
Here am I forty-five and I've never had an offer. ***Chorus***

I can cook and I can sew, I can keep the house right tidy
Rise up in the morning and get the breakfast ready
There's nothing in this wide world would make me half so cheery
As a wee fat man who would call me his own dearie. ***Chorus***

Oh come landsman or come townsman, come tinker or come tailor
Come fiddler, come dancer, come ploughman or come sailor
Come rich man, come poor man, come fool or come witty
Come any man at all who would marry me for pity. ***Chorus***

Oh well I'm away to home for there's nobody heeding
There's nobody heeding to poor old Annie's pleading
For I'm away home to my own wee-bit garret
If I can't get a man then I'll surely get a parrot! ***Chorus***

Bundoran, Donegal

Removal of CD

Carefully remove the CD from the CD sleeve.
Your CD can be stored in the CD sleeve, which is permanently fixed to the book cover, so that you can keep it safely with the book at all times.
Do not attempt to remove the CD sleeve from the cover of the book as it will result in damage to the book.

www.goganbooks.com